I0839984

Homeland Security, Federal Emergency Management Agency

How to Survive a Terrorist Attack – Become Prepared for a Bomb Threat or Active Shooter Assault

Madison & Adams Press 2019

Reading suggestions (available from Madison & Adams Press as Print & eBook)

U.S. Department of Defense
Counter Sniper Handbook - Eliminate the Risk with the Official US Army Manual

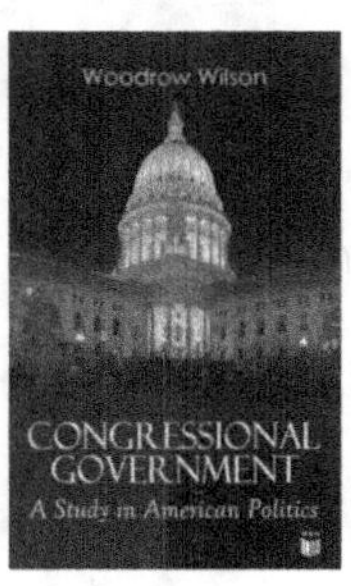

Woodrow Wilson
Congressional Government: A Study in American Politics

Charles Eastman
The Life of Charles Eastman OhiyeS'a: Indian Boyhood & From the Deep Woods to Civilization (Volume 1&2)

John Stuart Mill, W. L. Courtney
ON LIBERTY - The Philosophy of Individual Freedom

Charles Oman
The History of Byzantine Empire

Homeland Security, Federal Emergency Management Agency

How to Survive a Terrorist Attack – Become Prepared for a Bomb Threat or Active Shooter Assault

Save Yourself and the Lives of Others - Learn How to Act Instantly, The Strategies and Procedures After the Incident, How to Help the Injured & Be Able to Provide First Aid

Madison & Adams Press, 2019. No claim to original U.S. Government Works and to texts licensed as Creative Commons CC BY-SA 3.0.
Contact info@madisonadamspress.com

ISBN 978-80-273-3377-6

This is a publication of Madison & Adams Press. Our production consists of thoroughly prepared educational & informative editions: Advice & How-To Books, Encyclopedias, Law Anthologies, Declassified Documents, Legal & Criminal Files, Historical Books, Scientific & Medical Publications, Technical Handbooks and Manuals. All our publications are meticulously edited and formatted to the highest digital standard. The main goal of Madison & Adams Press is to make all informative books and records accessible to everyone in a high quality digital and print form.

Contents

Executive Summary

Recent improvised explosive device (IED) and active shooter incidents reveal that some traditional practices of first responders need to be realigned and enhanced to improve survivability of victims and the safety of first responders caring for them. This Federal, multi-disciplinary first responder guidance translates evidence-based response strategies from the U.S. military's vast experience in responding to and managing casualties from IED and/or active shooter incidents and from its significant investment in combat casualty care research into the civilian first responder environment. Additionally, civilian best practices and lessons learned from similar incidents, both in the United States and abroad, are incorporated into this guidance. Recommendations developed in this paper fall into three general categories: hemorrhage control, protective equipment (which includes, but is not limited to, ballistic vests, helmets, and eyewear), and response and incident management.

Hemorrhage Control

1. First responders should incorporate tourniquets and hemostatic agents as part of treatment for severe bleeding (if allowed by protocol). Tourniquets and hemostatic agents have been demonstrated to be quick and effective methods for preventing exsanguination from extremity wounds (tourniquets) and other severe external bleeding (hemostatic agents).
2. First responders should develop and adopt evidence-based standardized training that addresses the basic, civilianized tenets of Tactical Combat Casualty Care (TCCC). Training should be conducted in conjunction with fire, emergency medical services (EMS), and medical community personnel to improve interoperability during IED and/or active shooter incidents.

Protective Equipment

1. First responders should develop inter-domain (EMS, fire, and law enforcement) Tactics, Techniques, and Procedures (TTPs) — including use of ballistic vests, better situational awareness, and application of concealment and cover concepts — and train first responders on them.
2. As technology improves, first responders should adopt proven protective measures (e.g., body armor) that have been demonstrated to reliably shield personnel from IED fragments and shock waves.
3. First responders, when dealing with either IED or active shooter incidents, must remain vigilant and aware of the potential risk posed by secondary IEDs or additional shooters.

Response and Incident Management

1. Local and state law enforcement and emergency services should institutionalize National Incident Management System (NIMS)-based command and control language through plans and exercises and during ongoing education and training.
2. Local and state emergency management, EMS, fire, and law enforcement personnel and receiving medical facilities should have interoperable radio and communications equipment.
3. Local, state and federal partners should consider expansion of Public Safety Answering/Access Point (PSAP) intake procedures to include information gathering vital to the initial response.
4. Training to improve first responder triaging precision is essential for dealing with IED and/or active shooter incidents.
5. There should be greater coordination among EMS, fire services, and law enforcement to work more effectively during IED and/or active shooter incidents. The dialogue should

focus on potential improvements or changes to the TTPs which have historically been used during law enforcement situations that involve a medical emergency (e.g., EMS waits until law enforcement secures the scene before they enter to render emergency care).

The recommendations presented — early, aggressive hemorrhage control; use of body armor and a more integrated response; and greater first responder interoperability — will help to save lives by mitigating first responder risk and by improving the emergent and immediate medical management of casualties encountered during IED and/or active shooter incidents.

Purpose

Recent improvised explosive device (IED) and active shooter incidents reveal that some traditional practices of first responders need to be realigned and enhanced — with an emphasis on early hemorrhage control and a more integrated response by first responders (i.e., emergency medical services [EMS], fire, law enforcement, and rescue personnel) — to improve survivability of victims and the safety of first responders caring for them.[1] At the request of first responders and first receivers (e.g., medical technicians, nurses, and physicians) who have encountered mass casualties from IEDs and/or active shooter incidents, this document was developed to provide guidance on how to better approach these incidents.

Responders should also consider the combination of both IEDs and active shooter incidents in an organized, complex attack (such as the Mumbai attacks in 2008) that requires both treatment and extraction of the injured from a still-hostile environment. The conditions during such tactical assaults in a civilian setting speak to the need for first responders and first receivers to adopt evidence-based hemorrhage control, risk evaluation, and casualty management measures in a potentially dangerous environment.

As a result of these developments, the Department of Homeland Security, in coordination with the Department of Defense (DoD), Department of Health and Human Services, Department of Justice, Department of Transportation, White House Office of Science and Technology Policy, and the National Security Staff, has developed recommendations for individuals who provide emergent and immediate medical management of casualties resulting from IEDs and/or active shooter incidents. Based on best practices and lessons learned, this document focuses on the medical response to IEDs and/or active shooter incidents with recommendations for hemorrhage control, protective equipment (which includes ballistic vests, helmets, and eyewear), and response and incident management.

General Information:

Improvised Explosive Device

An **improvised explosive device (IED)** is a bomb worldwide constructed and deployed in ways other than in conventional military action. It may be constructed of conventional military explosives, such as an artillery round, attached to a detonating mechanism. IEDs are commonly used as **roadside bombs**.

IEDs are generally seen in heavy terrorist actions or in asymetric unconventional warfare by guerrillas or commando forces in a theater of operations. In the second Iraq War, IEDs were used extensively against US-led invasion forces and by the end of 2007 they had become responsible for approximately 63% of coalition deaths in Iraq. They are also used in Afghanistan by insurgent groups, and have caused over 66% of coalition casualties in the 2001–present Afghanistan War.

IEDs were also used extensively by cadres of the rebel Tamil Tiger (LTTE) organization against military targets in Sri Lanka.

Background

The term comes from the British Army in the 1970s, after the Provisional Irish Republican Army (IRA) used bombs made from agricultural fertilizer and Semtex smuggled from Libya to make highly effective boobytrap devices or remote-controlled bombs.

An IED is a bomb fabricated in an improvised manner incorporating destructive, lethal, noxious, pyrotechnic, or incendiary chemicals and designed to destroy or incapacitate personnel or vehicles. In some cases, IEDs are used to distract, disrupt, or delay an opposing force, facilitating another type of attack. IEDs may incorporate military or commercially sourced explosives, and often combine both types, or they may otherwise be made with homemade explosives (HME).

An IED has five components: a switch (activator), an initiator (fuse), container (body), charge (explosive), and a power source (battery). An IED designed for use against armoured targets such as personnel carriers or tanks will be designed for armour penetration, by using a shaped charge that creates an explosively formed penetrator. IEDs are extremely diverse in design and may contain many types of initiators, detonators, penetrators, and explosive loads.

Antipersonnel IEDs typically also contain fragmentation-generating objects such as nails, ball bearings or even small rocks to cause wounds at greater distances than blast pressure alone could. IEDs are triggered by various methods, including remote control, infrared or magnetic triggers, pressure-sensitive bars or trip wires (victim-operated). In some cases, multiple IEDs are wired together in a daisy chain to attack a convoy of vehicles spread out along a roadway.

IEDs made by inexperienced designers or with substandard materials may fail to detonate, and in some cases, they actually detonate on either the maker or the emplacer of the device. Some groups, however, have been known to produce sophisticated devices constructed with components scavenged from conventional munitions and standard consumer electronics components, such as mobile phones, consumer-grade two-way radios, washing machine timers, pagers, or garage door openers. The sophistication of an IED depends on the training of the designer and the tools and materials available.

IEDs may use artillery shells or conventional high-explosive charges as their explosive load as well as homemade explosives. However, the threat exists that toxic chemical, biological, or radioactive (dirty bomb) material may be added to a device, thereby creating other life-threatening effects beyond the shrapnel, concussive blasts and fire normally associated with bombs. Chlorine liquid has been added to IEDs in Iraq, producing clouds of chlorine gas.

A **vehicle-borne IED**, or **VBIED**, is a military term for a car bomb or truck bomb but can be any type of transportation such as a bicycle, motorcycle, donkey (DBIED), etc. They are typically employed by insurgents, and can carry a relatively large payload. They can also be detonated from a remote location. VBIEDs can create additional shrapnel through the destruction of the vehicle itself and use vehicle fuel as an incendiary weapon. The act of a person's being in this vehicle and detonating it is known as an SVBIED suicide.

Of increasing popularity among insurgent forces in Iraq is the house-borne IED, or HBIED from the common military practice of clearing houses; insurgents rig an entire house to detonate and collapse shortly after a clearing squad has entered.

Historical Use

The fougasse was improvised for centuries, eventually inspiring factory-made land mines. Ernst Jünger mentions in his war memoir the systematic use of IEDs and booby traps to cover the retreat of German troops at the Somme region during the First World War. Another early example of coordinated large-scale use of IEDs was the Belarusian Rail War launched by Belarusian guerrillas against the Germans during World War II. Both command-detonated and delayed-fuse IEDs were used to derail thousands of German trains during 1943-1944.

Afghanistan

Starting six months before the invasion of Afghanistan by the USSR on 27 December 1979, the Afghan Mujahideen were supplied with large quantities of military supplies. Among those supplies were many types of anti-tank mines. The insurgents often removed the explosives from several foreign anti-tank mines, and combined the explosives in tin cooking-oil cans for a more powerful blast. By combining the explosives from several mines and placing them in tin cans, the insurgents made them more powerful, but sometimes also easier to detect by Soviet sappers using mine detectors. After an IED was detonated, the insurgents often used direct-fire weapons such as machine guns and rocket-propelled grenades to continue the attack.

Afghan insurgents operating far from the border with Pakistan did not have a ready supply of foreign anti-tank mines. They preferred to make IEDs from Soviet unexploded ordnance. The devices were rarely triggered by pressure fuses. They were almost always remotely detonated. Since the 2001 invasion of Afghanistan, the Taliban and its supporters have used IEDs against NATO and Afghan military and civilian vehicles. This has become the most common method of attack against NATO forces, with IED attacks increasing consistently year on year.

U.S. Marines with Explosive Ordnance Disposal (EOD) destroy an Improvised Explosive Device (IED) cache in southern Afghanistan in June 2010.

According to a report by the Homeland Security Market Research in the USA, the number of IEDs used in Afghanistan had increased by 400 percent since 2007 and the number of troops killed by them by 400 percent, and those wounded by 700 percent. It has been reported that IEDs are the number one cause of death among NATO troops in Afghanistan.

A brigade commander said that sniffer dogs are the most reliable way of detecting IEDs. However, statistical evidence gathered by the US Army Maneuver Support Center at Fort

Leonard Wood, MO shows that the dogs are not the most effective means of detecting IEDs. The U.S. Army's 10th Mountain Division was the first unit to introduce explosive detection dogs in southern Afghanistan. In less than two years the dogs discovered 15 tons of illegal munitions, IED's, and weapons.

In July 2012 it was reported that "sticky bombs", magnetically adhesive IED's that were prevalent in the Iraq War, showed up in Afghanistan.

ISAF troops stationed in Afghanistan and other IED prone areas of operation would commonly "BIP" (Blow In Place) IED's and other explosives that were considered too dangerous to defuse.

India

IEDs are increasingly being used by Maoists in India.

On 13 July 2011, three IEDs were used by the Insurgency in Jammu and Kashmir to carry out a coordinated attack on the city of Mumbai, killing 19 people and injuring 130 more.

On 21 February 2013, two IEDs were used to carry out bombings in the Indian city of Hyderabad. The bombs exploded in Dilsukhnagar, a crowded shopping area of the city, within 150 metres of each other.

On 17 April 2013, Two kilos of explosives used in Bangalore bomb blast at Malleshwaram area, leaving 16 injured and no fatalities. Intelligence sources have said the bomb was an Improvised Explosive Device or IED.

On 21 May 2014, Indinthakarai village supporters of the Kudankulam Nuclear Power Plant were targeted by opponents using over half a dozen crude "country-made bombs". It was further reported that there had been at least four similar bombings in Tamil Nadu during the preceding year.

On 28 December 2014, a minor explosion took place near the Coconut Grove restaurant at Church Street in Bangalore on Sunday around 8:30 pm. One woman was killed and another injured in the blast.

During the 2016 Pathankot attack, several casualties came from IEDs.

Iraq

In the 2003-2011 Iraq War, IEDs have been used extensively against Coalition forces and by the end of 2007 they have been responsible for at least 64% of Coalition deaths in Iraq.

Beginning in July 2003, the Iraqi insurgency used IEDs to target invading coalition vehicles. According to the Washington Post, 64% of U.S deaths in Iraq occurred due to IEDs. A French study showed that in Iraq, from March 2003 to November 2006, on a global 3,070 deaths in the US-led invading coalition soldiers, 1,257 were caused by IEDs, i.e. 41%. That is to say more than in the "normal fights" (1027 dead, 34%). Insurgents now use the bombs to target not only invading coalition vehicles but Iraqi police as well.

Common locations for placing these bombs on the ground include animal carcasses, soft drink cans, and boxes. Typically they explode underneath or to the side of the vehicle to cause the maximum amount of damage; however, as vehicle armor was improved on military vehicles, insurgents began placing IEDs in elevated positions such as on road signs, utility poles, or trees, in order to hit less protected areas.

IEDs in Iraq may be made with artillery or mortar shells or with varying amounts of bulk or homemade explosives. Early during the Iraq war, the bulk explosives were often obtained from stored munitions bunkers to include stripping landmines of their explosives.

Despite the increased armor, IEDs have been killing military personnel and civilians with greater frequency. May 2007 was the deadliest month for IED attacks thus far, with a reported 89 of the 129 invading coalition casualties coming from an IED attack. According to the Pentagon, 250,000 tons (out of 650,000 tons total) of Iraqi heavy ordnance were looted, providing a large supply of ammunition for the insurgents.

In October 2005, the UK government charged that Iran was supplying insurgents with the technological know-how to make shaped charge IEDs. Both Iranian and Iraqi government officials denied the allegations.

During Iraqi Civil War (2014-present) ISIS makes extensive use of suicide VBIEDs, often driven by children, elderly and disabled.

United Kingdom/Republic of Ireland

Throughout The Troubles, the Provisional IRA made extensive use of IEDs in their 1969-97 campaign. They used barrack buster mortars and remote controlled IEDs. Members of the IRA developed and counter-developed devices and tactics. IRA bombs became highly sophisticated, featuring anti-handling devices such as a mercury tilt switch or microswitches. These devices would detonate the bomb if it was moved in any way. Typically, the safety-arming device used was a clockwork Memopark timer, which armed the bomb up to 60 minutes after it was placed by completing an electrical circuit supplying power to the anti-handling device. Depending on the particular design (e.g., boobytrapped briefcase or car bomb) an independent electrical circuit supplied power to a conventional timer set for the intended time delay, e.g. 40 minutes. However, some electronic delays developed by IRA technicians could be set to accurately detonate a bomb weeks after it was hidden, which is what happened in the Brighton hotel bomb attack of 1984. Initially, bombs were detonated either by timer or by simple command wire. Later, bombs could be detonated by radio control. Initially, simple servos from radio-controlled aircraft were used to close the electrical circuit and supply power to the detonator. After the

British developed jammers, IRA technicians introduced devices that required a sequence of pulsed radio codes to arm and detonate them. These were harder to jam.

Roadside bombs were extensively used by the IRA. Typically, a roadside bomb was placed in a drain or culvert along a rural road and detonated by remote control when British security forces vehicles were passing. As a result of the use of these bombs, the British military stopped transport by road in areas such as South Armagh, and used helicopter transport instead to avoid the danger.

Most IEDs used commercial or homemade explosives, although the use of Semtex-H smuggled in from Libya in the 1980s was also common from the mid-1980s onward. Bomb Disposal teams from 321 EOD manned by Ammunition Technicians were deployed in those areas to deal with the IED threat. The IRA also used secondary devices to catch British reinforcements sent in after an initial blast as occurred in the Warrenpoint Ambush. Between 1970 and 2005, the IRA detonated 19,000 improvised explosive devices (IEDs) in the Northern Ireland and Britain, an average of one every 17 hours for three and a half decades, arguably making it "the biggest terrorist bombing campaign in history".

In the early 1970s, at the height of the IRA campaign, the British Army unit tasked with rendering safe IEDs, 321 EOD, sustained significant casualties while engaged in bomb disposal operations. This mortality rate was far higher than other high risk occupations such as deep sea diving, and a careful review was made of how men were selected for EOD operations. The review recommended bringing in psychometric testing of soldiers to ensure those chosen had the correct mental preparation for high risk bomb disposal duties.

The IRA came up with ever more sophisticated designs and deployments of IEDs. Booby Trap or Victim Operated IEDs (VOIEDs), became commonplace. The IRA engaged in an on-going battle to gain the upper hand in electronic warfare with remote controlled devices. The rapid changes in development led 321 EOD to employ specialists from DERA (now Dstl, an agency of the MOD), the Royal Signals, and Military Intelligence. This approach by the British army to fighting the IRA in Northern Ireland led to the development and use of most of the modern weapons, equipment and techniques now used by EOD Operators throughout the rest of the world today.

The bomb disposal operations were led by Ammunition Technicians and Ammunition Technical Officers from 321 EOD, and were trained at the Felix Centre at the Army School of Ammunition.

Lebanon

The Lebanese National Resistance Front, the Popular Front for the Liberation of Palestine, other resistance groups in Lebanon, and later Hezbollah, made extensive use of IEDs to resist Israeli forces after Israel's invasion of Lebanon in 1982. Israel withdrew from Beirut, Northern Lebanon, and Mount Lebanon in 1985, whilst maintaining its occupation of Southern Lebanon. Hezbollah frequently used IEDs to attack Israeli military forces in this area up until the Israeli withdrawal, and the liberation of Lebanon in May 2000.

One such bomb killed Israeli Brigadier General Erez Gerstein on February 28, 1999, the highest-ranking Israeli to die in Lebanon since Yekutiel Adam's death in 1982.

Also in the 2006 War in Lebanon, a Merkava Mark II tank was hit by a pre-positioned Hezbollah IED, killing all 4 IDF servicemen on board, the first of two IEDs to damage a Merkava tank.

Libya

Homemade IEDs are used extensively during the post-civil war violence in Libya, mostly in the city of Benghazi against police stations, cars or foreign embassies.

Nepal

IEDs were also widely used in the 10-years long civil war of the Maoists in Nepal, ranging from those bought from illicit groups in India and China, to self-made devices. Typically used devices were pressure cooker bombs, socket bombs, pipe bombs, bucket bombs, etc. The devices were used more for the act of terrorizing the urban population rather than for fatal causes, placed in front of governmental offices, street corners or road sides. Mainly, the home-made IEDs were responsible for destruction of majority of structures targeted by the Maoists and assisted greatly in spreading terror among the public.

Nigeria

Boko Haram are using IEDs during their insurgency.

Pakistan

Taliban and other insurgent groups use IEDs against police, military, security forces, and civilian targets.

Russia

IEDs have also been popular in Chechnya, where Russian forces were engaged in fighting with rebel elements. While no concrete statistics are available on this matter, bombs have accounted for many Russian deaths in both the First Chechen War (1994-1996) and the Second (1999-2008).

Somalia

Al Shabaab is using IEDs during the Somalia Civil War.

Syria

During the Syrian Civil War, militant insurgents were using IEDs to attack buses, cars, trucks and tanks. Additionally, the Syrian Air Force has used barrel bombs to attack targets in cities and other areas. Such barrel bombs consist of barrels filled with high explosives, oil, and shrapnel, and are dropped from helicopters.

ISIS is using VBIEDs also in Syria, including during 2017 Aleppo suicide car bombing.

United States

In the 1995 Oklahoma City bombing, Timothy McVeigh and Terry Nichols built an IED with ammonium nitrate fertilizer, nitromethane, and stolen commercial explosives in a rental truck, with sandbags used to concentrate the explosive force in the desired direction. McVeigh detonated it next to the Alfred P. Murrah Federal Building, killing 168 people, 19 of whom were children.

In January 2011, a shaped pipe bomb was discovered and defused at a Martin Luther King Jr. memorial march in Spokane, Washington. The FBI said that the bomb was specifically designed to cause maximum harm as the explosive device was, according to the *Los Angeles Times*, packed with fishing weights covered in rat poison, and may have been racially motivated. No one was injured during the event.

On April 15, 2013, as the annual Boston Marathon race was concluding, two bombs were detonated seconds apart close to the finish line. Initial FBI response indicated suspicion of IED pressure cooker bombs.

On September 17-19, 2016, several explosions occurred in Manhattan and New Jersey. The sources of the explosions were all found to be IEDs of various types, such as pressure cooker bombs and pipe bombs.

Vietnam

IEDs were used during the Vietnam War by the Viet Cong against land- and river-borne vehicles as well as personnel. They were commonly constructed using materials from unexploded American ordnance. Thirty-three percent of U.S. casualties in Vietnam and twenty-eight percent of deaths were officially attributed to mines; these figures include losses caused by both IEDs and commercially manufactured mines.

The *Grenade in a Can* was a simple and effective booby trap. A hand grenade with the safety pin removed and safety lever compressed was placed into a container such as a tin can, with a length of string or tripwire attached to the grenade. The can was fixed in place and the string was stretched across a path or doorway opening and firmly tied down. In alternative fashion, the string could be attached to the moving portion of a door or gate. When the grenade was pulled out of the can by a person or vehicle placing tension on the string, the spring-loaded safety lever would release and the grenade would explode.

The *rubber band grenade* was another booby trap. To make this device, a Viet Cong guerrilla would wrap a strong rubber band around the spring-loaded safety lever of a hand grenade and remove the pin. The grenade was then hidden in a hut. American and South Vietnamese soldiers would burn huts regularly to prevent them from being inhabited again, or to expose foxholes and tunnel entrances, which were frequently concealed within these structures. When a hut with the booby trap was torched, the rubber band on the grenade would melt, releasing the safety lever and blowing up the hut. This would often wound the soldiers with burning bamboo and metal fragments. This booby trap was also used to destroy vehicles when the modified grenade was placed in the fuel tank. The rubber band would be eaten away by the chemical action of the fuel, releasing the safety lever and detonating the grenade.

Another variant was the *Mason jar grenade*. The safety pin of hand grenades would be pulled and the grenades would be placed in glass Ball Mason jars, which would hold back the safety lever. The safety lever would release upon the shattering of the jar and the grenade would detonate. This particular variant was popular with helicopter warfare, and were used as improvised anti-personnel cluster bombs during air raids. They were easy to dump out of the flight door over a target, and the thick Ball Mason glass was resistant to premature shattering. They could also be partially filled with gasoline or jellied gasoline, Napalm, to add to their destructive nature.

Yemen

Houthis are using IEDs against Saudi-led coalition and Hadi's forces during Yemeni Civil War (2015–present) and Saudi-led intervention in Yemen.

Types

By Warhead

The *Dictionary of Military and Associated Terms* (JCS Pub 1-02) includes two definitions for improvised devices: improvised explosive devices (IED) and improvised nuclear device (IND). These definitions address the *Nuclear* and *Explosive* in CBRNe. That leaves chemical, biological and radiological undefined. Four definitions have been created to build on the structure of the JCS definition. Terms have been created to standardize the language of first responders and members of the military and to correlate the operational picture.

Explosive

A device placed or fabricated in an improvised manner incorporating destructive, lethal, noxious, pyrotechnic, or incendiary chemicals and designed to destroy, incapacitate, harass, or distract. It may incorporate military stores, but is normally devised from non-military components.

Explosively formed penetrator/projectiles (EFPs)

IEDs have been deployed in the form of explosively formed projectiles (EFP), a special type of shaped charge that is effective at long standoffs from the target (50 meters or more), however they are not accurate at long distances. This is because of how they are produced. The large "slug" projected from the explosion has no stabilization because it has no tail fins and it does not spin like a bullet from a rifle. Without this stabilization the trajectory can not be accurately determined beyond 50 meters. An EFP is essentially a cylindrical shaped charge with a machined concave metal disc (often copper) in front, pointed inward. The force of the shaped charge turns the disc into a high velocity slug, capable of penetrating the armor of most vehicles in Iraq.

Improvised explosive device in Iraq. The concave copper shape on top defines an explosively formed penetrator/projectile

Directionally focused charges

Directionally focused charges (also known as directionally focused fragmentary charges) are very similar to EFPs, with the main difference being that the top plate is usually flat and not concave. It also is not made with machined copper but much cheaper cast or cut metal. The contents of the canister are usually nuts, bolts, ball bearings and other similar shrapnel products and explosive.

Chemical

A device incorporating the toxic attributes of chemical materials designed to result in the dispersal of these toxic chemical materials for the purpose of creating a primary patho-physiological toxic effect (morbidity and mortality), or secondary psychological effect (causing fear and behavior modification) on a larger population. Such devices may be fabricated in a completely improvised manner or may be an improvised modification to an existing weapon.

Biological

A device incorporating biological materials designed to result in the dispersal of vector borne biological material for the purpose of creating a primary patho-physiological toxic effect (morbidity and mortality), or secondary psychological effect (causing fear and behavior modification) on a larger population. Such devices are fabricated in a completely improvised manner.

Incendiary

A device making use of exothermic chemical reactions designed to result in the rapid spread of fire for the purpose of creating a primary patho-physiological effect (morbidity and mortality), or secondary psychological effect (causing fear and behavior modification) on a larger population or it may be used with the intent of gaining a tactical advantage. Such devices may be fabricated in a completely improvised manner or may be an improvised modification to an existing weapon. A common type of this is the Molotov cocktail.

Radiological

A speculative device incorporating radioactive materials designed to result in the dispersal of radioactive material for the purpose of area denial and economic damage, and/or for the purpose of creating a primary patho-physiological toxic effect (morbidity and mortality), or secondary psychological effect (causing fear and behavior modification) on a larger population. Such devices may be fabricated in a completely improvised manner or may be an improvised modification to an existing nuclear weapon. Also called a Radiological Dispersion Device (RDD) or "dirty bomb".

Nuclear

Improvised nuclear device of most likely gun-type or implosion-type.

Nanotechnology can theoretically be used to develop miniaturised laser-triggered pure fusion weapon that will be easier to produce than conventional nuclear weapons and could be used in terrorist attacks.

By delivery mechanism

Car

A vehicle may be laden with explosives, set to explode by remote control or by a passenger/driver, commonly known as a car bomb or vehicle-borne IED (VBIED, pronounced *vee-bid*). On occasion the driver of the car bomb may have been coerced into delivery of the vehicle under duress, a situation known as a proxy bomb. Distinguishing features are low-riding vehicles with excessive weight, vehicles with only one passenger, and ones where the interior of the vehicles look as if they have been stripped down and built back up. Car bombs can carry thousands of pounds of explosives and may be augmented with shrapnel to increase fragmentation. The U.S. State Department has published a guide on car bomb awareness.

ISIS has used truck bombs with devastating effects.

Artillery shells and gasoline cans discovered in the back of a pick-up truck in Iraq

Boat

Boats laden with explosives can be used against ships and areas connected to water. An early example of this type was the Japanese Shinyo suicide boats during World War II. The boats were laden with explosives and attempted to ram Allied ships, sometimes successfully, having sunk or severely damaged several American ships by war's end. Suicide bombers used a boat-borne IED to attack the USS Cole, US and UK troops have also been killed by boat-borne IEDs in Iraq.

Animal

Monkeys and war pigs were used as incendiaries around 1000 AD. More famously the "anti-tank dog" and "bat bomb" were developed during World War II. In recent times, a two-year-old child and seven other people were killed by explosives strapped to a horse in the town of Chita in Colombia The carcasses of certain animals were also used to conceal explosive devices by the Iraqi insurgency.

Collar

IEDs strapped to the necks of farmers have been used on at least three occasions by guerrillas in Colombia, as a way of extortion. American pizza delivery man Brian Douglas Wells was killed in 2003 by an explosive fastened to his neck, purportedly under duress from the maker of the bomb. In 2011 a schoolgirl in Sydney, Australia had a suspected collar bomb attached to her by an attacker in her home. The device was removed by police after a ten-hour operation and proved to be a hoax.

Suicide

Suicide bombing usually refers to an individual wearing explosives and detonating them in order to kill others including themselves, a technique pioneered by LTTE (Tamil Tigers). The bomber will conceal explosives on and around their person, commonly using a vest (or possibly a prosthetic) and will use a timer or some other trigger to detonate the explosives. The logic behind such attacks is the belief that an IED delivered by a human has a greater chance of achieving success than any other method of attack. In addition, there is the psychological impact of fighters prepared to deliberately sacrifice themselves for their cause.

Surgically implanted

In May 2012 American counter-terrorism officials leaked their acquisition of documents describing the preparation and use of surgically implanted improvised explosive devices. The devices were designed to evade detection. The devices were described as containing no metal, so they could not be detected by X-rays.

Security officials referred to bombs being surgically implanted into suicide bombers' "love handles".

According to *The Daily Mirror* UK security officials at MI-6 asserted that female bombers could travel undetected carrying the explosive chemicals in otherwise standard breast implants. The bomber would blow up the implanted explosives by injecting a chemical trigger.

Improvised Rocket

In 2008, rocket-propelled IEDs, dubbed *Improvised Rocket Assisted Munitions, Improvised Rocket Assisted Mortars* and (*IRAM*) by the military, came to be employed in numbers against U.S. forces in Iraq. They have been described as propane tanks packed with explosives and powered by 107 mm rockets. They are similar to some Provisional IRA barrack buster mortars. New types of IRAMs including Volcano IRAM and Elephant Rockets, are used during Syrian Civil War.

Improvised Mortar

Improvised mortar has been used by many insurgent groups including during civil war in Syria and Boko Haram insurgency. IRA used improvised mortars called barrack busters.

Improvised Artillery

Improvised artillery including *hell cannons* is used by rebel forces during Syrian Civil War.

By trigger mechanism

Wire

Command-wire improvised, explosive devices (CWIED) use an electrical firing cable that affords the user complete control over the device right up until the moment of initiation.

Radio

The trigger for a radio-controlled improvised explosive device (RCIED) is controlled by radio link. The device is constructed so that the receiver is connected to an electrical firing circuit and the transmitter operated by the perpetrator at a distance, A signal from the transmitter causes the receiver to trigger a firing pulse that operates the switch. Usually the switch fires an initiator; however, the output may also be used to remotely arm an explosive circuit. Often the transmitter and receiver operate on a matched coding system that prevents the RCIED from being initiated by spurious radio frequency signals or jamming. An RCIED can be triggered from any number of different mechanisms including car alarms, wireless door bells, cell phones, pagers and encrypted GMRS radios.

Mobile Phone

A radio-controlled IED (RCIED) incorporating a mobile phone that is modified and connected to an electrical firing circuit. Mobile phones operate in the UHF band in line of sight with base transceiver station (BTS) antennae sites. In the common scenario, receipt of a paging signal by phone is sufficient to initiate the IED firing circuit.

Victim-operated

Victim-operated improvised explosive devices (VOIED), also known as booby traps, are designed to function upon contact with a victim. VOIED switches are often well hidden from the victim or disguised as innocuous everyday objects. They are operated by means of movement. Switching methods include tripwire, pressure mats, spring-loaded release, push, pull or tilt. Common forms of VOIED include the under-vehicle IED (UVIED), improvised landmines, and mail bombs.

Infrared

The British accused Iran and Hezbollah of teaching Iraqi fighters to use infrared light beams to trigger IEDs. As the occupation forces became more sophisticated in interrupting radio signals around their convoys, the insurgents adapted their triggering methods. In some cases, when a more advanced method was disrupted, the insurgents regressed to using uninterruptible means, such as hard wires from the IED to detonator; however, this method is much harder to effectively conceal. It later emerged however, that these "advanced" IEDs were actually old IRA technology. The infrared beam method was perfected by the IRA in the early '90s after it acquired the technology from a botched undercover British Army operation. Many of the IEDs being used against the invading coalition forces in Iraq were originally developed by the British Army who unintentionally passed the information on to the IRA. The IRA taught their techniques to the Palestine Liberation Organisation and the knowledge spread to Iraq.

Counterefforts

Counter-IED efforts are done primarily by military, law enforcement, diplomatic, financial, and intelligence communities and involve a comprehensive approach to countering the threat networks that employ IEDs, not just efforts to defeat the devices themselves.

Detection and disarmament

Because the components of these devices are being used in a manner not intended by their manufacturer, and because the method of producing the explosion is limited only by the science and imagination of the perpetrator, it is not possible to follow a step-by-step guide to detect and disarm a device that an individual has only recently developed. As such, explosive ordnance disposal (IEDD) operators must be able to fall back on their extensive knowledge of the first principles of explosives and ammunition, to try and deduce what the perpetrator has done, and only then to render it safe and dispose of or exploit the device. Beyond this, as the stakes increase and IEDs are emplaced not only to achieve the direct effect, but to deliberately target IEDD operators and cordon personnel, the IEDD operator needs to have a deep understanding of tactics to ensure he is neither setting up any of his team or the cordon troops for an attack, nor walking into one himself. The presence of chemical, biological, radiological, or nuclear (CBRN) material in an IED requires additional precautions. As with other missions, the EOD operator provides the area commander with an assessment of the situation and of support needed to complete the mission.

A U.S. Marine in Iraq shown with a robot used for disposal of buried devices

Military and law enforcement personnel from around the world have developed a number of render-safe procedures (RSPs) to deal with IEDs. RSPs may be developed as a result of direct experience with devices or by applied research designed to counter the threat. The supposed effectiveness of IED jamming systems, including vehicle- and personally-mounted systems, has caused IED technology to essentially regress to command-wire detonation methods. These are physical connections between the detonator and explosive device and cannot be jammed. However, these types of IEDs are more difficult to emplace quickly, and are more readily detected.

Military forces and law enforcement from India, Canada, United Kingdom, Israel, Spain, and the United States are at the forefront of counter-IED efforts, as all have direct experience in dealing with IEDs used against them in conflict or terrorist attacks. From the research and development side, programs such as the new Canadian Unmanned Systems Challenge will bring student groups together to invent an unmanned device to both locate IEDs and pinpoint the insurgents.

Active Shooter

Active killer or **active shooter** names the perpetrator of a type of mass murder marked by rapidity, scale, randomness and suicide.

The United States Department of Homeland Security defines the *active shooter* as "an individual actively engaged in killing or attempting to kill people in a confined and populated area; in most cases, active shooters use firearms(s) [sic] and there is no pattern or method to their selection of victims." Most incidents occur at locations in which the killers find little impediment in pressing their attack. Locations are generally described as *soft targets*, that is, they carry limited security measures to protect members of the public. In most instances, shooters commit suicide, are shot by police, or surrender when confrontation with responding law enforcement becomes unavoidable. According to New York City Police Department (NYPD) statistics, 46 percent of active shooter incidents are ended by the application of force by police or security, 40 percent end in the shooter's suicide, 14 percent of the time the shooter surrenders and, in less than 1 percent of cases, the violence ends with the attacker fleeing, although the report provides no formal definition of the relevant terms and, as a result, the scope of its statistical findings is somewhat ungrounded.

Terminology

In police training manuals, the police response to an active shooter scenario is different from hostage rescue and barricaded suspect situations. Police officers responding to an armed barricaded suspect often deploy with the intention of containing the suspect within a perimeter, gaining information about the situation, attempting negotiation with the suspect, and waiting for specialist teams like SWAT.

If police officers believe that a gunman intends to kill as many people as possible before committing suicide, they may use a tactic like Immediate Action Rapid Deployment.

The terminology "active shooter" is critiqued by some academics. There have been several mass stabbings that have high casualty counts, for instance in Belgium (Dendermonde nursery attack), Canada (2014 Calgary stabbing), China (2008 Beijing Drum Tower stabbings), Japan (Osaka School Massacre), and Pennsylvania (Franklin Regional High School stabbing). Ron Borsch recommends the phrase "rapid mass murder".

Tactical implications

Active shooters do not negotiate, killing as many civilians as possible, often to gain notoriety. Active shooters generally do not lie in wait to battle responding law enforcement officers. Few law enforcement officers have been injured responding to active shooter incidents; fewer still have been killed. As noted, more often than not, when the prospect of confrontation with responding law enforcement becomes unavoidable, the active shooter commits suicide. And when civilians — even unarmed civilians — resist, the active shooter crumbles.

Borsch sums up the matter neatly:

> In reality (not theory), and round numbers, rapid mass murder has been aborted primarily by a single courageous actor. 50% have been UNARMED [civilians], 25% were armed [civilians], and the remainder have been police officers (also primarily initiated by a SOLO officer).

Borsch's statistical analysis recommends a tactic: aggressive action. For law enforcement, the tactical imperative is to respond and engage the killer without delay — the affected orthodoxy of cumbersome team formations fails to answer the rapid temporal dynamics of active shooter events and fails to grasp the nature of the threat involved. For civilians, when necessity or obligation calls, the tactical mandate is to attack the attacker — a strategy that has proved successful across a range of incidents from Norina Bentzel (William Michael Stankewicz) in Pennsylvania and Bill Badger in Arizona (2011 Tucson shooting) to David Benke in Colorado.

Taxonomy

The active shooter is a mass murderer. Not all mass murderers are active shooters. Noting the similarities and differences among several types of mass murder will help to isolate and define what is meant by the term "active shooter".

Mass murderers defy traditional criminal categorization. The goal of the mass murderer is neither to defend nor appropriate turf or territory, neither to initiate himself into nor elevate his status within a criminal organization. The mass murderer does not kill for drugs or money. The serial killer is one kind of mass murderer. He claims many lives in multiple events across time. The events are discontinuous, punctuated by "a cooling-off period". By contrast, the active shooter claims many lives in a single event along a compressed frame of time. In practice, this appears to carry a corollary: broadly, the serial killer seeks anonymity; the active shooter, notoriety. Repetition through multiple events across time answers the pathology of the serial killer. Savage as they are, his acts are not designed to excite publicity. The serial killer will conceal a corpse or bury evidence. He wants to kill again. By contrast, the active shooter seeks infamy through slaughter. He means to fuse his name forever to a place, a date, an event. Thus, his acts are designed to maximize publicity. Accordingly, he (generally) plans no escape.

The serial killer murders at close quarters, delighting in experiencing the horror of his victims as he shares their space. In his distorted estimation, his victims "mean" something to him, and he may secure keepsakes from victims to memorialize the "relationship". The active shooter also murders at close quarters. He delights in experiencing the horror of his victims as he shares their space. Crucially, however, while the victims of the serial killer "mean" something to him, to the active shooter they mean nothing. The active shooter moves rapidly from one victim to the next.

Modell speculates that the contrast is rooted in the peculiar form of abuse each suffers. The serial killer is a victim of physical/sexual/emotional abuse. Such abuse is administered at length, over time, by those who, by relation or connection, should care for the abused. The serial killer, after a manner, models this behavior. The active shooter is a victim of bullying. Though bullying may persist over time, it is delivered in discrete, relatively short-lived acts, often by multiple actors with no special relation or connection to the abused. The active shooter, after a manner, models this behavior.

A portrait of the active shooter may be sharpened by contrasting him with another type of mass murderer, the ideological killer. The Oklahoma City bombing exemplifies the type: in 1995, a man with ties to a disorganized militia movement detonated a truck bomb in front of the Alfred P. Murrah Building in downtown Oklahoma City, and the resulting blast ended 168 lives while wounding 680.

The ideological killer is driven by adherence to ethico-political or religious orthodoxy. His actions are an expression of that orthodoxy. By contrast, while the active shooter may conceive of himself as "making a statement" of sorts, his motives appear more personal and desultory.

Like the active shooter, the ideological killer plans multiple murders within the confines of a single event. But the active shooter seeks to experience the horror of his victims at close quarters. The ideological killer does not. He kills at a distance. He plants explosive devices or takes up position as a sniper. Killing at a distance suits his primary motive — the expression of adherence to an abstract orthodoxy. For the ideological killer, victims are of incidental significance. He need not "know" them, as the serial killer must, nor experience their horror, as the active shooter must. For the ideological killer, abstraction is reality, the individual but a construct in an interminable struggle of dogmas.

Since he is motivated by adherence to orthodoxy, the ideological killer typically seeks notoriety for his cause through carnage. While the active shooter too seeks notoriety, and while he too maps a careful plan of the event, there is a crucial difference in the pursuit. The ideological killer generally means to elude capture, to live beyond the event (as does the serial killer). The active shooter merges his identity with the event and sees nothing beyond.

Integrating the elements elicited by comparison and contrast, the "active shooter (killer)" may be defined as a mass murderer who kills (or attempts to kill) at close-quarters, in multiples, at random in a single, planned event.

Causation

Accounts of why active shooters do what they do vary. Some contend that the motive, at least proximately, is vengeance. Others argue that bullying breeds the problem, and indeed, the Active Shooter generally is a victim of bullying, directly or derivatively. Still others such as Grossman and DeGaetano argue that the pervasiveness of violent imagery girding modern culture hosts the phenomenon.

As an ultimate explanation, the vengeance theory must fail, for it cannot adequately account for the randomness of the killing. By any ordinary interpretation of the term "vengeance", one seeks to redress a perceived wrong against the one who wronged — not against a random set of individuals most of whom carry no connection to the killer. Likewise, bullying and violent imagery may be elements of an overall account, but neither suffices as an ultimate explanation. Many suffer bullying. Few of those bullied commit mass murder. And if violent imagery has become a staple of the culture, *a fortiori*, all are exposed to it. Yet few commit mass murder.

Some argue that a particular interpretation of the world, a conscious or subconscious ontology, accounts for the phenomenon. They argue that the active shooter lives in a world of victims and victimizers, that all are one or the other. The ontology accommodates no nuance, no room between the categories for benevolence, friendship, decency, nor indeed, for a mixture of good and bad. His interpretation of the world may grow out of or be fed by bullying or violent imagery (hence the common obsession with violent movies, books or video games), but it is the absolutist interpretation of his world that drives him both to kill and to die.

"The world conceived by the active killer is a dark dialectic of victim and victimizer. His impoverished ontology brooks no nuance, admits no resolution. The two categories, isolated and absolute, exhaust and explain his world. And the peculiar logic driving the dialectic yields a fatal inference: in a world of victims and victimizers, success means victimization."

Take an Active Role in Your Own Safety:

Explosions

Terrorists have frequently used explosive devices as one of their most common weapons. Terrorists do not have to look far to find out how to make explosive devices; the information is readily available in books and other information sources. The materials needed for an explosive device can be found in many places including variety, hardware, and auto supply stores. Explosive devices are highly portable using vehicles and humans as a means of transport. They are easily detonated from remote locations or by suicide bombers.

Conventional bombs have been used to damage and destroy financial, political, social, and religious institutions. Attacks have occurred in public places and on city streets with thousands of people around the world injured and killed.

Parcels that should make you suspicious:

- Are unexpected or from someone unfamiliar to you.
- Have no return address, or have one that can't be verified as legitimate.
- Are marked with restrictive endorsements such as "Personal," "Confidential," or "Do not X-ray."
- Have protruding wires or aluminum foil, strange odors, or stains.
- Show a city or state in the postmark that doesn't match the return address.
- Are of unusual weight given their size, or are lopsided or oddly shaped.
- Are marked with threatening language.
- Have inappropriate or unusual labeling.
- Have excessive postage or packaging material, such as masking tape and string.
- Have misspellings of common words.
- Are addressed to someone no longer with your organization or are otherwise outdated.
- Have incorrect titles or titles without a name.
- Are not addressed to a specific person.
- Have hand-written or poorly typed addressess.

Take Protective Measures

If you receive a telephoned bomb threat, you should do the following:
- Get as much information from the caller as possible.
- Keep the caller on the line and record everything that is said.
- Notify the police and the building management.

If there is an explosion, you should:

- Get under a sturdy table or desk if things are falling around you. When they stop falling, leave quickly, watching for obviously weakened floors and stairways. As you exit from the building, be especially watchful of falling debris.
- Leave the building as quickly as possible. Do not stop to retrieve personal possessions or make phone calls.
- Do not use elevators.

Once you are out:

- Do not stand in front of windows, glass doors, or other potentially hazardous areas.
- Move away from sidewal ks or streets to be used by emergency officials or others still exiting the building.

If you are trapped in debris:

- If possible, use a flashlight to signal your location to rescuers.
- Avoid unnecessary movement so you don't kick up dust.
- Cover your nose and mouth with anything you have on hand. (Dense-weave cotton material can act as a good filter. Try to breathe through the material.)
- Tap on a pipe or wall so rescuers can hear where you are.
- If possible, use a whistle to signal rescuers.
- Shout only as a last resort. Shouting can cause a person to inhale dangerous amounts of dust.

Active Shooter Incident

Recent national tragedies remind us that the risk is real: an active shooter incident can happen in any place at any time. The best ways to make sure you and your loved ones stay safe are to prepare ahead of time and be ready. Taking a few steps now and mentally rehearsing what to do can help you react quickly when every second counts.

TAKE AN ACTIVE ROLE IN YOUR OWN SAFETY NOW

NOW
PREPARE

- Sign up for active shooter training
- If you see something suspicious, say something
- Know community response plans
- Identify the exits and good places to hide
- Learn and practice first aid skills and use of tourniquets

- Run

- Hide

- Fight

You may need to use more than one option

AFTER
BE SAFE

- Help law enforcement
- Seek out medical help
- Help others survive
- Seek help to cope with psychological trauma

NOW
PREPARE

- Sign up for active shooter training.

- If you see suspicious activity, let an authority know right away.
- Many places like houses of worship, workplaces, and schools have plans in place to help you respond safely. Ask about these plans and get familiar with them. If you participate in an active shooter drill, talk to your family about what you learn and how to apply it to other locations.
- When you visit a building like a shopping mall or health care facility, take time to identify two nearby exits. Get in the habit of doing this.
- Map out places to hide. Solid doors with locks, rooms without windows, and heavy furniture like large filing cabinets and desks make good hiding places.
- Sign up for first aid and tourniquet training.

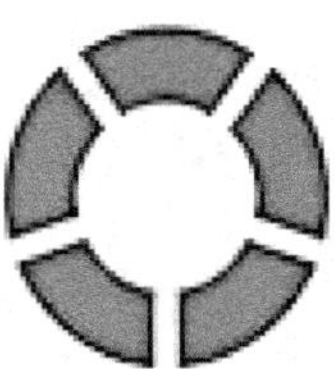

DURING
SURVIVE

- RUN. Getting away from the shooter or shooters is the top priority. Leave your things behind and run away. If safe to do so, warn others nearby. Call 911 when you are safe. Describe each shooter, their locations, and weapons.
- HIDE. If you can't get away safely, find a place to hide. Get out of the shooter's view and stay very quiet. Silence your electronic devices and make sure they won't vibrate. Lock and block doors, close blinds, and turn off the lights. Don't hide in groups — spread out along walls or hide separately to make it more difficult for the shooter. Try to communicate with police silently — like through text messages or by putting a sign in an exterior window. Stay in place until law enforcement gives you the all clear.
- FIGHT. Your last resort when you are in immediate danger is to defend yourself. Commit to your actions and act aggressively to stop the shooter. Ambushing the shooter together with makeshift weapons such as chairs, fire extinguishers, scissors, and books can distract and disarm the shooter.

AFTER
BE SAFE

- Keep hands visible and empty.
- Know that law enforcement's first task is to end the incident, and they may have to pass injured along the way.
- Follow law enforcement instructions and evacuate in the direction they come from.

- Consider seeking professional help for you and your family to cope with the long-term effects of the trauma.

HELPING THE WOUNDED

Take care of yourself first, and then you may be able to help the wounded before first responders arrive:

- If the injured are in immediate danger, help get them to safety.
- While you wait for first responders to arrive, provide first aid — apply direct pressure to wounds and use tourniquets if you have been trained to do so. Turn wounded people onto their sides if they are unconscious and keep them warm.

First Responder for Improving Survivability in Improvised Explosive Device and/or Active Shooter Incidents

Background:

Defining First Responders

In this guidance, the term "first responder" refers to a diverse set of persons who, from the earliest stages of an incident, are critical to managing and caring for people who are injured by an IED and/or active shooter incident. The term "first responder" does not imply a formal credential, certification, limitation, or capacity. First responders may include bystanders, law enforcement, and EMS and fire personnel. EMS and fire personnel typically encompass the traditional scopes of practice as identified in the National Highway Traffic Safety Administration's National Scope of Practice Model (2007). Levels of medical credentialing and quantity of resources for EMS and fire personnel can vary greatly depending on the EMS delivery model. Bystanders, who likely will be on scene prior to EMS, fire, or law enforcement arrival, may or may not have some form of medical training, and those volunteering at the site of an attack may be poorly equipped and at risk for additional explosions, ballistic threats, and hazardous environments. In some areas, the jurisdiction involved may benefit from volunteer services such as Community Emergency Response Teams (CERTs), the Emergency System for Advance Registration of Volunteer Health Professionals, or the Medical Reserve Corps (MRC). These volunteers are organized and trained to provide community support to natural disasters, accidents, and attacks. In the United States, the role of first receivers is frequently associated with "brick and mortar" medical facilities that often do not have the protective equipment necessary to face potential hostile conditions or hazardous environments.

Defining the Threat

Single or multiple IED events targeting civilians and/or first responders represent an ongoing and growing threat from domestic and foreign individuals or groups. In the United States between 1970 and 2011, excluding the 9/11 attacks, four of six attacks with more than 50 injuries, and 22 of 45 attacks with more than five injuries, involved IEDs.[2] IED "types" likely to cause mass casualties include "leave behind" parcels, backpacks, or luggage placed in crowded environments; "suicide vests" or "suicide belts"; and especially vehicle bombs. Traumatic injuries may result from IEDs in many ways: from penetration or blunt force trauma caused by the fragmentation and high-velocity projection of pieces of its immediate container (e.g., a metal pipe, box, or pressure cooker); from items intentionally added to compound the number of projectiles (e.g., ball bearing, nails, etc.); from incidental fragmentation and projection of material or debris from a larger container or vessel the IED is placed within (e.g., a vehicle trunk or trash bin); by collateral fragmentation and/or projection of material affected by blast, such as windows, walls, or other objects in the vicinity; and by blast overpressure itself, without any projectiles at all. Where an IED is placed — indoors or out, near or far from other objects — will influence its blast effects. Understanding the numerous ways in which IEDs can cause injuries and how the environment plays a role in exacerbating or mitigating their blast effects is critical to increasing survivability when unexploded IEDs are present or secondary IEDs are suspected. In addition to causing life and limb threatening injuries, these events generate confusion, uncertainty, and fear at the scene that ripple throughout the receiving medical system.

Active shooter incidents represent a similar, and increasing, threat to responders. Like IED events, active shooter incidents require extraordinary efforts on the part of first responders. Though these incidents typically end within a short period of time, some may involve large, complex locations and require many hours to clear suspected hazards after the initial event.

Military Lessons Learned and Civilian Adaptation

Experience in combat casualty care gained by the U.S. military during the wars in Iraq and Afghanistan, augmented by the DoD's investment in trauma care and surgical research, has resulted in a vast amount of knowledge pertaining to the management of explosive injury and gunshot wounds, with a particular focus on life-threatening external hemorrhage control.

Tactical Combat Casualty Care

Information on wounds suffered by U.S. Army soldiers in Vietnam between July 1967 and June 1979 found that of those killed in action, 9 percent died from extremity hemorrhage, 5 percent died from tension pneumothorax, and 1 percent died from airway obstruction. These findings, that one-sixth of combat casualties result from three types of wounds that are easily treated in the field, led to the development in the late 1990s of Tactical Combat Casualty Care (TCCC) — a set of prehospital trauma care guidelines for battlefield use that focus on the most common causes of treatable exsanguination deaths in combat.

Tactical Emergency Casualty Care

Recognizing how this military experience could apply to civilian high-threat medical operations, an independent group of civilian first responders in 2011 founded the Committee for Tactical Emergency Casualty Care (C-TECC)[3] to develop guidelines that translate military medical lessons learned from the battlefield to civilian crisis response. The resulting Tactical Emergency Casualty Care (TECC) guidelines are a set of evidence-based best practice recommendations for casualty management during high-threat civilian tactical and rescue operations that are based on military TCCC principles but account for differences in the civilian environment, resources allocation, patient population, and scope of practice. It is important to emphasize that C-TECC is an independent civilian entity and not necessarily endorsed by the DoD. TECC is the civilian evolution of TCCC, written to address the subtle differences in the civilian operational environment.[4]

A collaborative group of public safety organizations — including fire, law enforcement, prehospital care, trauma care, and the military — convened in Hartford, Connecticut, in the spring of 2013 to develop consensus regarding strategies to increase survivability in mass-casualty shootings (commonly referred as the Hartford Consensus). The group states that "no one should die from uncontrolled bleeding" and developed the acronym THREAT to address these situations:

> Threat suppression,
> Hemorrhage control,
> Rapid Extrication to safety,
> Assessment by medical providers, and
> Transport to definitive care.[5]

In its "Call to Action," this group of experts advocates that uninjured or minimally injured victims can act as rescuers; law enforcement should utilize external hemorrhage control as a core skill; EMS, fire, and rescue response must be more fully integrated and their traditional role limitations revised; and existing trauma systems should be used to optimize seamless care.

Concerned international and national first responder associations, such as the International Association of Chiefs of Police, International Association of Fire Fighters, International Association of Fire Chiefs, National Association of Emergency Medical Technicians, and the National Tactical Officers Associations, have shown great interest in this topic, and many have published position statements. The fire associations state that "common tactics, common communications capabilities and a common lexicon for seamless, effective operations" are required and "integrated and coordinated planning, policies, training and team building prior to the incident will ensure effective and successful response." Additionally, the National Tactical Officers Association (NTOA) states that there is a need for all police officers to have basic Tactical Emergency Medical Support (TEMS) medical training in order to potentially save the lives of victims, bystanders, police officers, and suspects in the event they are wounded.

NTOA has also stated that there is no single model for providing care during law enforcement operations and that TEMS basic principles should be considered core law enforcement skills relevant to all police operations, as NTOA "supports the efforts of the Committee for Tactical Emergency Casualty Care (C-TECC) and others to foster the development of standardized taxonomy and evidence based clinical practice guidelines tailored to the law enforcement mission."[6]

The following is a list of select TCCC/TECC interventions that have potential applicability in civilian trauma care systems following an IED and/or active shooter event:

- 1. The use of tourniquets to control extremity hemorrhage.
- 2. The use of hemostatic gauze to control bleeding from sites not amenable to tourniquet.
- 3. he use of a nasopharyngeal airway for patients without maxillofacial or neck trauma.
- 4. ositioning of a casualty in a recovery posture if feasible for conscious patients with maxillofacial trauma and bleeding into the airway.
- 5. Spinal precautions when feasible for patients with blunt but not penetrating trauma.
- 6. Intravenous (IV) access is not routinely required in the initial phase of treatment but can be performed by those with appropriate training and oversight.

The following additional interventions may be performed by those with advanced life support (ALS) training and capabilities:

- 7. Surgical airway if "sit up and lean forward" posture not possible in those with face/neck trauma.
- 8. Intraosseous (IO) access for medications or fluids when IV not successful or possible IO access is not routinely required in the initial phase of treatment.
- 9. IV morphine, oral transmucosal fentanyl citrate lozenges, and ketamine for analgesia.

Lessons learned from the military's recent combat experiences, and their civilian C-TECC counterparts, are incorporated within this guidance.

En Route Care

It is important to emphasize that emergency medical care activities should not stop as a casualty is evacuated. In fact, the military's experience demonstrates that continuation or escalation of these measures is critical in reducing mortality during prehospital care. While there is a need to understand how these military experiences in prehospital patient care can be leveraged to decrease morbidity (illness or injury) and mortality (death) in the civilian setting, the ability to translate the military's findings related to on-site and en route care to the civilian setting has not been fully demonstrated.

Hospital-Based Measures

The military's combat casualty care research on hospital-based management of patients with severe explosionrelated injuries is documented in a Balad Air Base Report from 2008[7] and on the Joint Trauma System Clinical Practice Guidelines website.[8]

One particularly successful strategy is damage control resuscitation (DCR), which demonstrated decreased mortality associated with the use of a blood component-based volume replacement compared to the use of crystalloid fluids for patients in shock. DCR is based on the balanced administration of thawed plasma, pRBCs, and platelets in severely injured patients instead of solutions such as normal saline and lactated ringers.[9][10][11][12] DCR also includes avoidance of hypothermia and pursuit of other measures to maximize oxygenation and reduce injurious factors in the blast-injured patient.

Morbidity and Mortality Prevention

There are three broad concepts related to the prevention or reduction of morbidity and mortality associated with an explosive event:

1. **Prevention:** Avoiding or thwarting the detonation is obviously the best way to avert IED-related injury, suffering, and death. Primary preventive measures, including improvements in preemptive mental health capabilities, an aware public who is able and willing to report suspicious pre-attack behaviors, tactical operations employed to render the device safe, and law enforcement intelligence gathering and threat-analysis capabilities, are beyond the scope of this paper. Preventing injuries of first responders and the public is of great importance. Safe distance from suspicious packages aids in preventing injuries from IEDs (see Figure 1).

2. **Mitigation:** This concept refers to actions taken to reduce the impact of an explosive event once an explosion has occurred, such as use of protective equipment and the placement of physical blast mitigation barriers or windows, and are sometimes referred to as secondary preventive measures. Some of the more sophisticated military protective equipment — including vests with ceramic plates, helmets, and protective undergarments — have been designed for and tested against mechanisms of injury resulting from explosive devices and ballistic threats. Most of the protective equipment available to civilian first responders, however, has been designed for protection from ballistic threats and was not designed, manufactured, or intended to provide protection from IEDs. It should also be noted that most protective equipment is focused on ballistic protection and may have unproven or limited value for mitigating fragmentation or blast overpressure, particularly for devices with larger net explosive weights, such as vehicle bombs. For protective equipment and barriers to be effective, they must be implemented proactively; they are of little use when the explosive event is random and enacted on an unsuspecting, unprotected group of individuals.

3. **Response:** This encompasses the initial treatment activities taken by first responders at the scene of injury and care provided while en route to the medical facility to prevent or reduce morbidity and mortality of individuals who have been injured by an explosive event.

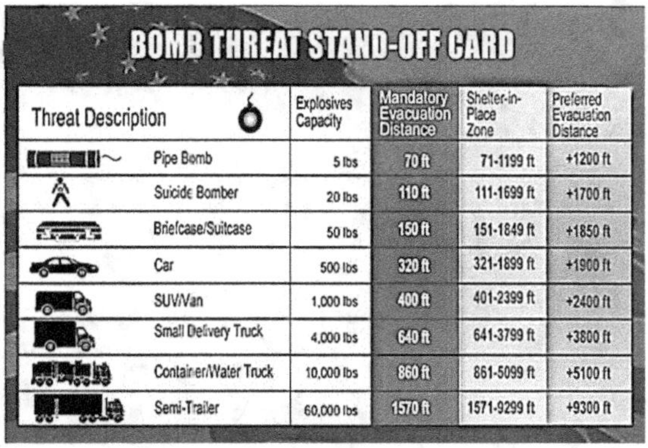

Threat Description		Explosives Capacity	Mandatory Evacuation Distance	Shelter-in-Place Zone	Preferred Evacuation Distance
	Pipe Bomb	5 lbs	70 ft	71-1199 ft	+1200 ft
	Suicide Bomber	20 lbs	110 ft	111-1699 ft	+1700 ft
	Briefcase/Suitcase	50 lbs	150 ft	151-1849 ft	+1850 ft
	Car	500 lbs	320 ft	321-1899 ft	+1900 ft
	SUV/Van	1,000 lbs	400 ft	401-2399 ft	+2400 ft
	Small Delivery Truck	4,000 lbs	640 ft	641-3799 ft	+3800 ft
	Container/Water Truck	10,000 lbs	860 ft	861-5099 ft	+5100 ft
	Semi-Trailer	60,000 lbs	1570 ft	1571-9299 ft	+9300 ft

Figure 1[13]

Published Civilian Experience

Civilian reports on the response to explosive incidents are primarily from non-U.S. centers and include those in Madrid, London, and Tel Aviv. [14] [15] [16] [17] [18] [19] [20] These, and a limited number of other reports, have provided valuable lessons learned regarding emergency response, triage, and surge requirements for an explosive incident. However, these studies provide little detail on prehospital, blood bank, operating room, health care provider, and hospital ward resource requirements following these events and are of limited applicability to emergency planning for similar events within the U.S. civilian sector.

Civilian response in the United States will vary depending on the geographic location, resources, and demographics of the incident. In most areas, the civilian response will be led by local law enforcement and emergency services. Routinely, requests for emergency assistance are obtained through Public Safety Answering/ Access Points (PSAP). The PSAP functions as the initial information collection point and can prove invaluable in coordinating the public sector response. Conversely, poor incident reporting and improperly dispatched response assets can lead to a delay in patient care.

Responders to active shooter incidents at Virginia Tech and in Aurora and Columbine in Colorado encountered various access denial schemes in the form of chemical munitions, fire, secondary IEDs, and mechanical obstructions. International IED and concerted attacks have utilized fire, smoke, chemical (chlorine), and security elements to challenge first responders and increase the damage and effectiveness of the attack.

CDC guidelines provide general strategies for the U.S. health care system in the event of a civilian terrorist bombing. [21] These CDC guidelines also include next steps such as forecasting necessary blood bank, operating room, and other associated hospital infrastructure resources. The CDC has also developed and disseminated courses and guidelines that address both the patient care and health care system challenges of medical response to civilian terrorist bombings. These materials were informed by U.S. civilian experts in prehospital and hospital care relating to mass casualty response, the DoD military medical experience, and those who led medical responses to terrorist bombings in Israel, Pakistan, London, Madrid, Mumbai, and Delhi. This material, designated the Terrorism Injuries: Information, Dissemination and Exchange (TIIDE) project, is available through the TIIDE Project website.

Active Shooter Incidents

Morbidity and Mortality Prevention

There are three broad concepts related to the prevention or reduction of morbidity and mortality associated with an active shooter incident:

1. **Prevention:** Avoiding or thwarting the active shooter incident is obviously the best way to avert active shooter-related injury, suffering, and death. Primary preventive measures, including improvements in preemptive mental health capabilities, an aware public who is able and willing to report suspicious pre-attack behaviors, and law enforcement active shooter intelligence gathering and threat-analysis capabilities, are beyond the scope of this paper.
2. **Mitigation:** This concept refers to actions taken to reduce the impact of an active shooter incident: evaluation of acceptable risk to facilitate provision of medical care for victims as soon as possible; use of protective equipment, such as ballistic vests, appropriate to the threat; and development of first responder TTPs that focus on active shooter scenarios. Other mitigation actions, such as a public trained in active shooter response or victim initiated mitigation measures, are outside of the scope of this paper.
3. **Response:** This encompasses the initial treatment activities taken by first responders at the scene of injury and care provided while en route to the medical facility to prevent or reduce morbidity and mortality of individuals who have been injured in an active shooter incident. Rapid first responder access to victims in an active shooter incident can make the difference between life and death, as the survival rate diminishes rapidly for seriously injured trauma victims the longer they must wait to receive definitive hospital care.[22]

Published Civilian Experience

Civilian reports on the response to active shooter incidents draw primarily from watershed domestic events such as the 1999 Columbine High School,[23] 2007 Virginia Tech,[24] and 2009 Fort Hood shootings, as well as the 2008 Mumbai terrorist attacks.[25] Studies from these and other primarily domestic events have provided valuable lessons regarding active shooter incident response policy, victim treatment, and first responder protective equipment recommendations. Lessons learned include concepts originally developed for and validated by the military during the conflicts in Iraq and Afghanistan that challenge some long-standing EMS principles of practice. Evaluation of these concepts seeks a balance between providing expeditious medical response for victims and ensuring effective risk management for first responder safety.

The current standard EMS response for an active shooter incident is to stage in a secure location until police mitigate the threat and secure the area. This can lead to a significant delay in providing medical care to the victims. Empirical evidence demonstrates that in an active shooter scenario, expeditious medical intervention, more than capability/capacity, was key to preventing loss of life.[26] Emerging alternatives to the "standby" policy suggest a level of first responder collaboration that allows EMS with appropriate protective equipment to quickly enter the incident scene with law enforcement officers in order to stabilize patients and reduce fatalities from readily treatable injuries. Variability exists in the training and deployment of law enforcement officers to rescue and care for victims. Law enforcement planners should employ strategies that enable all law enforcement officers to provide lifesaving care until additional resources can be moved forward.

Studies examining the weapons used during active shooter incidents, and the patterns of morbidity and mortality of these incidents, indicate that civilian active shooter scenarios present similar injuries and conditions to those seen in combat (in decreasing order of mortality): extremity hemorrhage, tension pneumothorax, or airway obstruction.[5] Each of these wounds is readily treatable with minimal supplies, but they are very time sensitive, and delay in treatment increases the risk of mortality. Because victims in an active shooter incident are more likely to suffer exsanguinating extremity wounds than airway injury, and because a person can bleed to death from a large arterial wound in 2-3 minutes while it may take 4-5 minutes to die from a compromised airway, C-TECC guidelines place control of external hemorrhage ahead of airway control — replacing the traditional ABC mnemonic (for airway, breathing, circulation) with MARCH (Massive hemorrhage control/Airway support/Respiratory threats/Circulation [prevent shock]/Hypothermia).

Hemorrhage Control

Control of External Hemorrhage in the Prehospital Setting

Tourniquet use on the battlefield has been demonstrated to be effective in decreasing the number of treatable exsanguination deaths due to extremity hemorrhage. There are a variety of tourniquets in use at present by the U.S. military. A recent comprehensive study of U.S. combat fatalities from 2001 to 2011 noted that the incidence of treatable exsanguination deaths related to extremity hemorrhage dropped from 7.8 percent in a previous study[27] to 2.6 percent by 2011,[28] a decrease attributed to the implementation of tourniquet use by U.S. forces. The number of U.S. lives saved in combat through the use of tourniquets alone is estimated to be between 1,000 and 2,000.[29] To be most effective, the tourniquet must be applied before the victim has lost enough blood to suffer hemorrhagic shock. Despite previous warnings about limb ischemia, there was no preventable loss of limbs resulting from tourniquet ischemia in a case study of 232 patients with tourniquets on 309 extremities.[30]

A shift from the traditional mantra of "tourniquet as a last resort" to "tourniquets are proven to save lives from treatable exsanguination injuries" is supported by evidence and will necessitate interoperable training across all domains of EMS, fire, and law enforcement.

Anatomic areas such as the neck, the groin, and the axilla contain large vascular structures and are not amenable to tourniquet placement. Studies at military medical research laboratories have evaluated the efficacy of hemostatic agents and found an advantage in the use of "packing hemostatic gauze" vs. granulated hemostatics.[31] [32] Junctional hemorrhage control devices such as the Combat Ready Clamp, the Abdominal Aortic Tourniquet, and the Junctional Emergency Treatment Tool may also be used to control hemorrhage from the groin area.

Direct pressure can also be used to control external bleeding, a technique that can work even with bleeding from major vessels such as the carotid or femoral arteries. Direct pressure must be applied consistently and with significant force to stop the bleeding and is best employed with the patient on a firm surface so that effective counterpressure is present. To control severe bleeding, direct pressure must be sustained until the casualty reaches an operating room, where surgical repair of the vessel can be performed.

Current guidelines and best practice recommendations for control of external hemorrhage and casualty management during civilian tactical and rescue operations are published on the C-TECC website.[33] The TCCC guidelines, which are the genesis for the TECC guidelines, were designed for military use and can be found on the National Association of Emergency Medical Technicians website.[34]

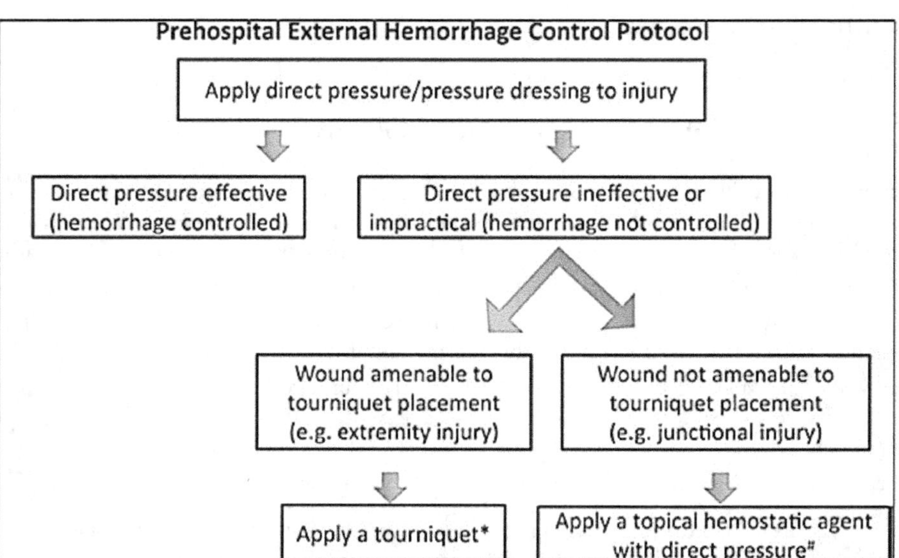

Prehospital External Hemorrhage Control Protocol
Apply direct pressure/pressure dressing to injury
Direct pressure effective (hemorrhage controlled)
Direct pressure ineffective or impractical (hemorrhage not controlled)
Wound amenable to tourniquet placement (e.g. extremity injury)
Wound not amenable to tourniquet placement (e.g. junctional injury)
Apply a tourniquet*
Apply a topical hemostatic agent with direct pressure#
*Use of tourniquet for extremity hemorrhage is strongly recommended if sustained direct pressure is ineffective or impractical; Use a commercially-produced, windlass, pneumatic, or ratcheting device, which has been demonstrated to occlude arterial flow and avoid narrow, elastic, or bungee-type devices; Utilize improvised tourniquets only if no commercial device is available ; Do not release a properly-applied tourniquet until the patient reaches definitive care
#Apply a topical hemostatic agent, in combination with direct pressure, for wounds in anatomic areas where tourniquets can not be applied and sustained direct pressure alone is ineffective or impractical; Only apply topical hemostatic agents in a gauze format that supports wound packing; Only utilize topical hemostatic agents which have been determined to be effective and safe in a standardized laboratory injury model

Figure 2[35]

Protective Equipment

Protective equipment (which includes ballistic vests, helmets, and eyewear) for both civilian first responders and the military is designed and tested according to anticipated threats, injury patterns, and existing technology. Historically, first responders have been primarily concerned with protective equipment to counter firearm and, to a certain extent, chemical, biological, radiological, and nuclear threats — not IEDs.

First Responders

The development of standards and the manufacturing of this protective equipment for first responders have only been available since the 1970s.[36][37] The 126 percent increase in police officer fatalities from 1966 to 1971 prompted the Department of Justice to develop and evaluate concealable soft body armor for daily use that would protect against ballistic threats while minimizing blunt trauma.[38][39] Handguns have historically been the most common threat to police officers,[40] but National Institute of Justice (NIJ) ballistic vest testing parameters follow trends in threats, and updated testing parameters are added based on new knowledge of vest performance and necessary test conditions.[41][42]

> First responder adoption of inter-domain tactics, techniques, and procedures that include the use of ballistic vests, better situational awareness, and the application of concealment and cover concepts ultimately increases first responder safety and allows quicker access to victims resulting in improved patient outcomes.

Currently there are five types of ballistic vests based on NIJ body armor standards. However, statistics from the Bulletproof Vest Partnership/Body Armor Safety Initiative[x] suggest that the majority of vests used by first responders are Type II and IIIA. Descriptions of the body armor standards are listed below, ordered by the level of protection. For instance, Type IIA provides protection against Type II and IIA threats, whereas Type III vests provide protection for Type IIA, Type II, and Type IIIA threats. All of the vests listed, with the exception of Types III and IV, are considered concealable body armor and designed to fit under a normal uniform shirt.[43] Some manufacturers also produce soft armor vests that accommodate "trauma packs", which are ballistic inserts added to a vest to provide added protection. These inserts are referred to as "in conjunction" designs and are similar to military ballistic inserts. These "in conjunction" designs must be threat level tested and labeled appropriately.[44] In other words, if a Type III vest provides Type III protection only in conjunction with a trauma pack, then the system's label must be marked accordingly. It is important to note that none of the five armor types have requirements to defeat IED fragments and therefore may not provide meaningful protection against either fragmentation or blast overpressure effects from IEDs. While other standards exist for protective suits used by public safety bomb technicians, the suits' weight, bulk, and limited numbers make them impractical for general use by first responders. The degree of protection civilian soft and rigid armors will provide against the complex shock and impact profiles that IEDs present is unknown. While available armor may provide some degree of protection from IED fragmentation, the fact it is unlikely to mitigate blast overpressure effects should be carefully considered by responders when involved in confirmed or suspected IED incidents, especially those in which larger net-explosive-weight IEDs such as vehicle bombs are confirmed or suspected.

NIJ Standard-0101.06 establishes five formal armor classification types:[45][46]

| Type IIA | protects against 9 mm; .40 S&W |
| Type II | protects against 9 mm; .357 Magnum |

Type IIIA	protects against.357 SIG; .44 Magnum
Type III	protects against Rifles; 7.62mm FMJ
Type IV	protects against Armor Piercing Rifles; .30 caliber AP

Army Testing of Personal Protective Equipment

Over the last several years, the U.S. Army Test and Evaluation Command (ATEC) has conducted thousands of ballistic tests of protective equipment, including individual pieces of equipment traditionally thought of as "body armor" (softer material vests containing hard armor plates), helmets, bomb suits, eye and face protection, extremity and pelvic protection, and concealable body armor. In a majority of these tests, the threats evaluated include 7.62mm to 9mm bullets, metallic fragments of various sizes and shapes, stab tests using both blade and pick threats, blast tests, and blunt trauma tests. Other types of testing are also conducted, such as durability, reliability, wearability, and suitability. Permission to review reports must be obtained from the test sponsor, since ATEC was contracted to conduct the assessment and is thus not the owner of the subsequent test data. All reports can be requested through the ATEC website.[47]

Response and Incident Management

The National Response Framework (NRF), which is built upon NIMS, describes the Nation's principles, roles and responsibilities, and coordinating structures for managing serious or large-scale incidents. Implementation of these elements, through training and education, helps mitigate risk by reinforcing the importance of unified command, interoperability, a standardized lexicon, and consideration of lessons learned from exercises and operations. Training and education on these elements also enable responders to adapt efficiently to evolving risks and allow for effective integration across all missions using a standards-based approach.

Greater collaboration and interoperability among EMS, fire services, and law enforcement during IED and/or active shooter events can save lives.

NIMS promotes the use of a common operating picture , interoperability of communications, and information management as essential principles in incident management. The ability of first responders to communicate with voice and/or data across disciplines and jurisdictions is central to improving the efficiency and effectiveness of incident response and emergency management activities. During initial response, the PSAP plays a particularly important role as the initial information link between those at the incident scene and EMS, fire responders, and law enforcement.

The United States Fire Administration (USFA) advocates that EMS, fire, and law enforcement personnel quickly establish unified command at scenes of IED and active shooter incidents.[48] EMS and fire personnel should be aware that law enforcement will aggressively and hastily send first arriving law enforcement personnel into the affected area of active shooter incidents to engage and neutralize the threat, to secure the perimeter to ensure the perpetrator does not escape, and to prevent inappropriate entry into the scene. The first arriving law enforcement personnel focused on neutralizing active shooter threats will typically not stop to render aid to injured bystanders, as the top priority is to stop further harm by addressing the threat. EMS and fire personnel, upon arrival to the scene, should move to the law enforcement command post, establish unified command as previously planned and exercised with law enforcement personnel, and anticipate active involvement in warm zone operations. A warm zone is an area of indirect threat, where law enforcement has either cleared or isolated the threat to a level of minimal or mitigated risk. This area can be considered clear but not secure.[49]

The USFA also advocates that EMS, fire, and law enforcement personnel must ensure that there are common tactics, communication capabilities, protocols, and procedures that are well practiced, exercised and known by all emergency services personnel before an IED and/or active shooter event occurs. The protocols and procedures should also address non-traditional roles of EMS and fire personnel. These roles include the use of properly trained, armored (not armed) medical personnel who are accompanied by law enforcement into areas of mitigated risk (warm zones). In these roles, life-saving care (i.e., hemorrhage control and airway management) and evacuation of the injured from the warm zone may help improve survivability of victims..[50]

Incorporation of EMS and fire into warm zones, where it is practiced, is at the discretion of the jurisdiction and is dependent on resources and relationships between all involved parties. There are various models and approaches for introducing EMS and fire personnel into warm zones, including the Rescue Task Force (RTF) model.[51] [52] RTFs, under the protection of law enforcement officers, render emergent and life-saving treatment at the basic life support level, stabilization, and removal of the injured victims of IED and/or active shooter incidents while wearing recommended ballistic protective equipment. Some RTF models include the use of one ALS provider per RTF, and other non-RTF models include the exclusive use of law enforcement for rapid patient removal of injured victims to awaiting EMS personnel in areas more distant from the threat, but still within the warm zone. Whichever model is used, the treatment rendered in the warm zone is limited to basic, urgent life-saving care focused on severe hemorrhage control and airway management.

Law enforcement agencies should train personnel to provide casualty care to establish a life-saving bridge to victims at an active shooter incident. Based on the immediacy of the threat and the geographic location of victims, law enforcement officers providing casualty care may offer the best chance for victim survival. Law enforcement programs that have robust rescue capabilities should train with supporting EMS programs and develop patient transfer measures that optimize patient survivability. A select few models have EMS and/ or fire personnel accompanying the law enforcement personnel into active (hot) zones. Regardless of the model adopted, the calculated and early incorporation of properly trained personnel (EMS, fire, and/or law enforcement) into warm zones allows critically injured victims to receive life-saving care in a more-timely manner.

Rendering life-saving care in warm zones (by EMS, fire, and/or law enforcement) is a relatively new paradigm that is supported by data. Historically, when EMS and fire personnel waited up to several hours before being permitted to enter scenes and render life-saving care, very few critical victims survived. The passage of that time resulted in the likely preventable loss of life for victims. The Wound Data and Munitions Effectiveness Team showed that 90 percent of Vietnam deaths occurred prior to definitive care, with 42 percent occurring within 5 to 30 minutes of injury.[53] Although the combat setting is not a direct translation into the civilian setting, the fact that most of the 42 percent of deaths were related to exsanguination from extremity wounds should be considered when deciding to incorporate trained personnel (EMS, fire, and/or law enforcement) into the scene to render life-saving hemorrhage control and airway management sooner rather than later.

Greater interoperability and collaborative education and training among EMS, fire services, and law enforcement during IED and/or active shooter events will enable first responders to conduct well-integrated and effective incident response and emergency management that can ultimately save more lives.

Responder Guidelines

The following guidelines for addressing hemorrhage control, protective equipment, and response and incident management were developed by the Federal Government through a collaborative evaluation of lessons learned from both military and civilian experience in reducing morbidity and mortality following an IED and/or active shooter incident.

Hemorrhage Control

1. 1. **First responders should incorporate tourniquets and hemostatic agents as part of treatment for severe bleeding (if allowed by protocol).**

Tourniquets and hemostatic agents have been demonstrated to be quick and effective methods for preventing exsanguination from extremity wounds (tourniquets) and other severe external bleeding (hemostatic agents). First responders should update training and educational content on tourniquets and hemostatic agents into a consistent standard within EMS, fire, and law enforcement domains.

1. 2. **First responders should adopt, develop training for, and operationalize the evidence-based guidelines of TECC. Training should be conducted in conjunction with EMS, fire, law enforcement, and medical community personnel to improve interoperability during IED and/or active shooter events.**

In order for the training to be most effective, it should be conducted from a systems perspective, involving EMS, fire, and law enforcement. This practice promotes better interoperability between EMS, fire, and law enforcement during IED and/or active shooter incidents, with the ultimate goal of saving lives.[54]

Response and Incident Management

> **1. 1. Local and state law enforcementand emergency services, should institutionalize NIMS-based command and control language and plans and exercises through ongoing education and training.**

Civilian response programs should develop joint policies, training, tactics, and communications that enhance the interoperability of all of the emergency services team (EMS, fire, emergency management, law enforcement, and others). Further information regarding NIMS and the NRF is available on the FEMA website.[55] [56]

> **1. 2. Local and state emergency management, EMS, fire, law enforcement and receiving medical facilities should have interoperable radio and communications equipment.**

Clear, concise communications and scene coordination between law enforcement and emergency services should be regularly tested through collaborative training and exercises. First responders should have the ability to talk across disciplines and jurisdictions via radio communications systems, exchanging voice and/or data with one another on demand, in real time, when needed, and as authorized. Law enforcement and emergency services leadership should explore when, where, and how to set up incident command posts, emergency operations centers, and briefing locations that are safe and secure from attempts to disrupt communications.

> **1. 3.   Local, state and federal partners need to consider expansion of PSAP intake procedures to include information gathering vital to the initial response.**

The PSAP is the initial information link between those at the incident scene and EMS and law enforcement responders. Development of joint PSAP, intake, dispatch, and communications plans, along with a common lexicon, will enhance first responder interoperability throughout all phases of these incidents.

> **1. 4. Training to improve first responder triaging precision and decrease unnecessary transport delays is essential for dealing with IED and/or active shooter incidents.**

Patients should be triaged for both priority of transport and for the destination. Under-triage can result in potentially life threatening conditions going unrecognized, resulting in delayed transport or transport to an inappropriate facility, while over-triaging risks having lower acuity patients overwhelm limited resources in higher-level medical facilities that could be better utilized treating more severely injured patients. With proper triage, the right patient will get to the right facility in the right time. First responders should routinely practice triage with a consideration for both medical priority of transport and capabilities of the destination treatment facility to maintain competency with the skill and knowledge.

> **1. 5. There should be greater coordination among EMS, fire services, and law enforcement to work more effectively during IED and/or active shooter incidents. The dialogue should focus on potential improvements or changes to the TTPs that have historically been used during law enforcement situations that involve a medical emergency (i.e., EMS waits until law enforcement secures the scene before they enter to render emergency care)**

The dialogue should focus on a mutual understanding of how the various first responder components approach IED and/or active shooter response operations, where areas of improvements and synergy might be found, and how evidence based clinical data and outcomes can be incorporated into future standards, education, and training. This may result in significant cultural and operational changes that contradict current practices.

EMS, fire, and law enforcement personnel must ensure that common tactics, communication capabilities, protocols, and procedures are well practiced, exercised, and known by all emergency services personnel before an IED and/or active shooter event occurs.. The protocols and procedures should also address nontraditional roles of EMS and fire personnel, including in warm zone operations, as previously described.

There are various models and approaches for introducing EMS and fire personnel into warm zones, as detailed earlier in this document. Regardless of the model adopted by the local jurisdiction, the calculated and early incorporation of properly trained EMS, fire, and law enforcement personnel into warm zones allows critically injured victims to receive life-saving care in a more timely manner.

Summary

This multi-disciplinary first responder guidance is the first of its kind to link the categories of prevention against IEDs and/or active shooter incidents to tangible, evidence-based response strategies designed to mitigate morbidity and mortality. This document builds on the U.S. military's vast experience in responding to and managing casualties from IEDs and/or active shooter incidents and on its significant investment in combat casualty care research, then filters it through civilian peer review literature and consensus-based best practices to distill practical, proven guidelines for effectively responding to these devastating events.

Current military practice and experience emphasize early and definitive control of external hemorrhage and have been estimated to have saved up to 2,000 American lives in Iraq and Afghanistan. Although the significance of life-threatening hemorrhage in civilian mass casualty has not been as clearly defined as it has in the military combat setting, until further data shows the need for a different medical emphasis, hemorrhage control should remain a priority. As such, aspects of this military experience have been translated to a number of civilian medical systems around the Nation. However, permeation of military and international lessons learned in the arena of medical response to explosive injury and/or active shooter incidents is incomplete. In most cases, the research conducted on protective equipment by the U.S. military can be translated to the civilian setting to assist in better protecting the workforce of first responders who are called upon to respond to IED and/or active shooter incidents. The focus on interoperability improvements between emergency services domains (EMS, fire, and law enforcement) will aid in saving lives impacted by IED and/or active shooter incidents.

To prepare for and reduce death and suffering following an IED detonation and/or active shooter event in a civilian environment, it is imperative that more widespread dissemination and adoption of lessons learned from these incidents, as well as the DoD's continuing combat medicine experience, occur within the U.S. civilian first responder and first receiver communities.

Threat-Based Scenarios

This section includes a list of scenarios and recommended medical and planning considerations. As the end-users of these scenarios, first responders are encouraged to incorporate details relevant to their local landmarks, response procedures, and practices. The purpose of the following scenarios is to guide first responder education and training efforts toward incorporation and institutionalization of the previous responder guidelines in a variety of likely IED and/or active shooter situations. These scenarios can be used individually as stand-alone resources, or they can be used in conjunction with the other scenarios provided. They are intended to be used for collaborative planning, training, and exercises with EMS, fire, and law enforcement resources together. Ideally, role playing should be done to help first responders better understand each other's processes and roles and the importance of unified command and interoperability.

Scenario 1: Large-Scale Terrorist/Insurgency Attack

Large-scale attack using an IED with over 100 pounds net explosive weight, producing mass casualties with the likelihood of overwhelming the response and receiving infrastructure. This scenario may include vehicleborne improvised explosive devices (VBIEDs).

EXAMPLE: You are called to the scene of a reported explosion at a train station (or other public location). Initial reports indicate that a truck drove around barriers and into the entrance of the facility and then detonated. 911 callers indicate that there are several dead and many others with multiple injuries — some extremely serious. You are the first arriving unit on the scene...

Expected Injury Patterns

For those who survive this event, injuries can include multiple amputees with pelvic/perineal components, penetrating thoraco-abdominal injuries, pulmonary contusions from closed space blasts, burns, TBI, including penetrating head injury, and neck trauma. While primary blast injuries can occur from both open space (e.g., roadside IED) and closed space (e.g., buildings, trains, and buses) bombings, it is especially common after closed space bombings.

Protective Equipment and Barriers

Secondary preventive measures include activities to prevent injuries once an explosion has occurred. Such measures may include barrier or structural walls that may protect or reduce injuries to bystanders and responders from blast and fragmentation injuries.[57] Secondary preventive measures also include use of ballistic protective equipment, although soft body armor and ceramic plate body armor may not protect against fragmentation or blast overpressure effects from IEDs. Most protective equipment is focused on ballistic protection and may have unproven or limited value for mitigating fragmentation or blast overpressure, particularly for devices with larger net explosive weights, such as vehicle bombs. For protective equipment and barriers to be effective, they must be implemented proactively; they are of little use when the explosive event is random and enacted on an unsuspecting, unprotected group of individuals. Ballistic protective equipment will also give some level of protection should an IED attack be combined with an active shooter event. Experience indicates attackers may plan to detonate secondary or subsequent IEDs that target first responders or receiving hospitals.

First responders should consider wearing some level of ballistic protective equipment. Considerations for first responder ballistic protective equipment should include what type of equipment is best suited for EMS and fire responders and when it should be worn (every shift, during times of high risk [e.g., on duty at a sports stadium], or just in response to IED events). It is critical that incident commanders base protective equipment and tactical movement guidance at the incident scene on a situational assessment of the IED risk, particularly when IEDs with significant net explosive weight are suspected or confirmed to be present. These types of IEDs, including vehicle bombs, may produce blast overpressure effects that would not be mitigated by typical protective equipment or available cover. A false sense of security among first responders could result if net explosive weight is not considered when determining protective equipment or tactical movement guidance to responders.

Protective Equipment Commonly Worn

Most law enforcement officers responding to the incident will be wearing Type II or IIIA bullet resistant vests, designed to stop bullets from most handguns, and shotgun pellets. Given the expected injuries, this level of protective equipment may not provide protection from blast overpressure and fragmentation, and extremities will be vulnerable. First responders other than law enforcement typically do not wear ballistic protective equipment. Civilians at public places will not be wearing any form of ballistic protective equipment.

Protective Equipment Risk Mitigation Considerations

The NIJ body armor standard specifies the ballistic threats that body armor must reliably protect against. This standard does not specify a requirement for ballistic resistant vests to

protect against fragmentation threats. The Type II or IIIA ballistic resistant vests that law enforcement officers are most commonly issued will likely not protect against fragmentation and blast overpressure effects from an IED threat. Use of Type IV body armor may increase the probability of protection against fragmentation and blast overpressure. However, further research and development is required to validate the performance of NIJ-approved body armor against fragmentation threats and to provide guidance on what level of protection should be worn to respond to this type of IED event.

Response and Incident Management Considerations

Maximize interoperability through existing MOUs/MOAs/SOPs, as well as through frequent exercises, planning, and training. These efforts will ultimately aid in reducing time from injury to treatment. During response, and while on the scene of the incident, use unified command with a mutual understanding of each responder's role (EMS, fire, and law enforcement). Strive to communicate on common frequencies and use standardized terminology. Ensure all responders (regardless of discipline — EMS, fire, and law enforcement) are trained and equipped to provide early, aggressive hemorrhage control; use protective equipment (which includes ballistic vests, helmets, and eyewear); and use integrated response and incident management.

Medical Response System

An IED detonation has the potential of instantly producing hundreds of casualties (there were over 700 casualties after the Oklahoma City bombing) with injuries that range across the entire spectrum of severity. A system-wide medical response to this event should be well-coordinated, incorporating the lessons learned from the military (both system and individual patient care) and experiences from domestic and international bombings. Unlike the management of routine emergencies, the response to IED incidents will be extraordinary for the Nation's trauma and EMS systems.

System-wide efforts should include activities ranging from self-care, buddy-care, and bystander care to proper and effective prehospital triaging and patient transport to get the right patients to the appropriate medical facilities in a swift and orderly manner, regardless of proximity. The efforts include prehospital emergency medical services, ground ambulances, rotary and fixed wing aircraft patient transport, designated trauma centers, hospitals, and rehabilitation facilities.

Prehospital Emergency Medical Services Considerations

Patient-Based Considerations: The last decade of war has seen significant advances in the ability of prehospital care to impact the mortality of combat wounds. The ability to stop life-threatening bleeding from extremity wounds has been demonstrated to reduce the number of treatable exsanguination deaths.

As IEDs have become a common source of wounding in the wars in Iraq and Afghanistan, and as the use of IEDs in the United States (the Boston Marathon bombing on April 15, 2013) has become a reality, civilian adoption of some military clinical practices that are a significant departure from traditional prehospital care should be considered:

- Aggressive hemorrhage control — including use of tourniquets and, where appropriate, hemostatic agents
- Aggressive airway management, including "sit up and lean forward" airway positioning
- Training all first responders in self-care, buddy care, and bystander care

System-Wide Implications

Experience from bombings occurring in other countries demonstrates common prehospital care system challenges, including multiple simultaneous attacks that cause an enormous number of casualties that exceed the available resources of EMS responders. The adoption of techniques that are suitable for use in self-care, buddy-care, bystander care, and care delivered by first responders is essential to extend the depth of responders available to provide immediate life-saving care.

EMS must rapidly and accurately triage casualties at the incident site and expeditiously transport those identified for "immediate care" into an appropriate hospital setting. It is imperative that pre-hospital triaging of wounded patients be as efficient and accurate as possible. Over-triage of patients over-taxes specialty centers that are designed to care for more significantly injured patients, while under-triaging of patients puts critically wounded patients into facilities that may not be able to provide the life-saving care needed. In addition to proper triage, care must be taken to regulate the transportation of casualties in order to direct victims to the hospital best suited for providing the necessary level of care for the type and severity of injuries they have sustained. Often the closest hospital is quickly overwhelmed by injured transported by ambulances, police cars, and privately owned vehicles, as well as the "walking wounded". Because the influx of patients to the nearest hospital is dictated by human behavior outside control of the system, the EMS system must recognize this likelihood and plan for redistribution of injured patients such that the closest hospital can return to maximum functionality as soon as possible. Incident managers should also anticipate the need to provide for safety and security with the arrival of injured persons' family members, the "psychologically shocked," and the media.

EMS providers must also be cognizant of patients who appear otherwise well (uninjured), but may have traumatic brain injuries, tympanic membrane damage, and/or internal hollow organ damage due to the blast effects of the explosion. These considerations should be reinforced through exercise, planning, protocols, and training.

Hospital-Based Trauma System Considerations

Hospital challenges experienced in foreign and domestic bombings include:

- Difficulty in acquiring information from the scene
- Maldistribution of patients (e.g., two of 15 hospitals receiving approximately 60 percent of casualties from the scene in one large-scale event)
- A requirement for large numbers of hospital medical personnel to adequately treat the wounded
- The need to implement mass casualty contingency plans at every point of care (e.g., radiology postponing imaging an ankle sprain to rule out a fracture)
- Concern that the hospital may be a target
- Activation of Mass Transfusion Protocols, based on scope of injuries
- Activation of staff augmentation/call back plans, based on scope of injuries
- Initiation of patient movement/transfer plans, based on scope of injuries

Medical leaders of responses to bombings have noted that in many cases the majority of the injured and dead from large events present at the hospital closest to the scene. Patients able to leave the scene may forego EMS triage and present at hospitals before more severely injured patients arrive. The large influx of patients may exceed the hospital's capability to provide care, resulting in a "functional collapse" from inability to meet the demand spike. When this occurs, there is a compelling need to redistribute patients.

Distribution of patients among hospitals, so that no one hospital exceeds its resources, is a key principle in addressing medical surge capacity following bombing attacks that result in significant casualties.

To address the large number of patients arriving at local facilities, local hospitals will need the swift assistance of incoming health care providers to assist with re-triage of the arriving casualties and the provision of appropriate services to patients. This influx will include additional doctors, nurses, medical specialists, such as blood bank technologists and respiratory therapists, mental health providers, and chaplains. In addition, there will likely be the need for law enforcement personnel to maintain order and security. In the hours immediately after the blast, these additional personnel will likely come from surrounding communities and may include health care professionals from beyond the local area. While pre-event planning for cross-town (local) hospital credentialing and privileging of responding health care professionals can be arranged with relative ease, the issue of expeditious out-of-state credentialing and privileging of medical professionals responding to natural or man-made disasters can be more challenging.

Patient Movement/Transfer Considerations

As the patient load builds at local hospitals, some of the critically injured patients should be moved to other medical care facilities to optimize patient care. This will include movement to Level-1 trauma centers and other hospitals to better balance inpatient bed, operating room, intensive care unit, and rehabilitation bed utilization. Depending on the locality of the blast, this may include moving patients to other communities or across state lines. Long-distance transport of acutely injured patients will likely require aeromedical evacuation capabilities.

Scenario 2: Medium-Scale Terrorist/Insurgency Attack

Medium-scale attack using an IED with between 5 and 100 pounds net explosive weight, producing a significant number of mass casualties with the potential of overwhelming the response and receiving infrastructure. This scenario may include vehicle-borne improvised explosive devices (VBIEDs).

EXAMPLE: You are called to respond to an explosion inside a large house of worship in your response area. The 911 center received multiple calls, and there are many reported deaths and significant injuries. Your unit is the first arriving unit to the scene...

Expected Injury Patterns

For those who survive this event, injuries can include single and double amputees, extremity vascular injuries, penetrating foreign body thoraco-abdominal injuries, potential TBI and penetrating head trauma, neck trauma, and pulmonary contusions from closed space blasts.

Protective Equipment and Barriers

Secondary preventive measures include activities to prevent injuries once an explosion has occurred. Such measures may include barrier or structural walls that may protect or reduce injuries to bystanders and responders from blast and fragmentation injuries.[58] Secondary preventive measures also include use of ballistic protective equipment, although soft body armor and ceramic plate body armor may not protect against fragmentation or blast overpressure effects from IEDs. Most protective equipment is focused on ballistic protection and may have unproven or limited value for mitigating fragmentation or blast overpressure, particularly for devices with larger net explosive weights, such as vehicle bombs. For protective equipment and barriers to be effective, they must be implemented proactively; they are of little use when the explosive event is random and enacted on an unsuspecting, unprotected group of individuals. Ballistic protective equipment will also give some level of protection should an IED attack be combined with an active shooter event. Experience indicates attackers may plan to detonate secondary or subsequent IEDs that target first responders or receiving hospitals.

First responders should consider wearing some level of ballistic protective equipment. Considerations for first responder ballistic protective equipment should include what type of equipment is best suited for EMS and fire responders and when it should be worn (every shift, during times of high risk [e.g., on duty at a sports stadium], or just in response to IED events). It is critical that incident commanders base protective equipment and tactical movement guidance at the incident scene on a situational assessment of the IED risk, particularly when IEDs with significant net explosive weight are suspected or confirmed to be present. These types of IEDs, including vehicle bombs, may produce blast overpressure effects that would not be mitigated by typical protective equipment or available cover. A false sense of security among first responders could result if net explosive weight is not considered when determining protective equipment or tactical movement guidance to responders.

Protective Equipment Commonly Worn

Most law enforcement officers responding to the incident will be wearing Type II or IIIA bullet resistant vests, designed to stop bullets from most handguns, and shotgun pellets. Given the expected injuries, this level of protective equipment may not provide protection from blast overpressure and fragmentation, and extremities will be vulnerable. First responders other than law enforcement typically do not wear ballistic protective equipment. Civilians at public places will not be wearing any form of ballistic protective equipment.

Protective Equipment Risk Mitigation Considerations

The NIJ body armor standard specifies the ballistic threats that body armor must reliably protect against. This standard does not specify a requirement for ballistic resistant vests to protect against fragmentation threats. The Type II or IIIA ballistic resistant vests that law enforcement officers are most commonly issued will likely not protect against fragmentation and blast overpressure effects from an IED threat. Use of Type IV body armor may increase the probability of protection against fragmentation and blast overpressure. However, further research and development is required to validate the performance of NIJ-approved body armor against fragmentation threats and to provide guidance on what level of protection should be worn to respond to this type of IED event.

Response and Incident Management Considerations

Maximize interoperability through existing MOUs/MOAs/SOPs, as well as through frequent exercises, planning, and training. These efforts will ultimately aid in reducing time from injury to treatment. During response, and while on the scene of the incident, use unified command with a mutual understanding of each responder's role (EMS, fire, and law enforcement). Strive to communicate on common frequencies and use standardized terminology. Ensure all responders (regardless of discipline — EMS, fire, law enforcement) are trained and equipped to provide early, aggressive hemorrhage control; use protective equipment (which includes ballistic vests, helmets, and eyewear); and use integrated response and incident management.

Medical Response System

An IED detonation has the potential of instantly producing hundreds of casualties (there were over 700 casualties after the Oklahoma City bombing) with injuries that range across the entire spectrum of severity. A system-wide medical response to this event should be well-coordinated, incorporating the lessons learned from the military (both system and individual patient care) and experiences from domestic and international bombings. Unlike the management of routine emergencies, the response to IED incidents will be extraordinary for the Nation's trauma and EMS systems.

System-wide efforts should include activities ranging from self-care, buddy-care, and bystander care to proper and effective prehospital triaging and patient transport to get the right patients to the appropriate medical facilities in a swift and orderly manner, regardless of proximity. The efforts include prehospital emergency medical services, ground ambulances, rotary and fixed wing aircraft patient transport, designated trauma centers, hospitals, and rehabilitation facilities.

Prehospital Emergency Medical Services Considerations

Patient-Based Considerations: The last decade of war has seen significant advances in the ability of prehospital care to impact the mortality of combat wounds. The ability to stop life-threatening bleeding from extremity wounds has been demonstrated to reduce the number of treatable exsanguination deaths.

As IEDs have become a common source of wounding in the wars in Iraq and Afghanistan, and as the use of IEDs in the United States (the Boston Marathon bombing on April 15, 2013) has become a reality, civilian adoption of some military clinical practices that are a significant departure from traditional prehospital care should be considered:

- Aggressive hemorrhage control — including use of tourniquets and, where appropriate, hemostatic agents
- Aggressive airway management, including "sit up and lean forward" airway positioning
- Training all first responders in self-care, buddy care, and bystander care

System-Wide Implications

Experience from bombings occurring in other countries demonstrates common prehospital care system challenges, including multiple simultaneous attacks that cause an enormous number of casualties that exceed the available resources of EMS responders. The adoption of techniques that are suitable for use in self-care, buddy-care, bystander care, and care delivered by first responders is essential to extend the depth of responders available to provide immediate life-saving care.

EMS must rapidly and accurately triage casualties at the incident site and expeditiously transport those identified for "immediate care" into an appropriate hospital setting. It is imperative that pre-hospital triaging of wounded patients be as efficient and accurate as possible. Over-triage of patients over-taxes specialty centers that are designed to care for more significantly injured patients, while under-triaging of patients puts critically wounded patients into facilities that may not be able to provide the life-saving care needed. In addition to proper triage, care must be taken to regulate the transportation of casualties in order to direct victims to the hospital best suited for providing the necessary level of care for the type and severity of injuries they have sustained. Often the closest hospital is quickly overwhelmed by injured transported by ambulances, police cars, and privately owned vehicles, as well as the "walking wounded". Because the influx of patients to the nearest hospital is dictated by human behavior outside control of the system, the EMS system must recognize this likelihood and plan for redistribution of injured patients such that the closest hospital can return to maximum functionality as soon as possible. Incident managers should also anticipate the need to provide for safety and security with the arrival of injured persons' family members, the "psychologically shocked," and the media.

EMS providers must also be cognizant of patients who appear otherwise well (uninjured), but may have traumatic brain injuries, tympanic membrane damage, and/or internal hollow organ damage due to the blast effects of the explosion. These considerations should be reinforced through exercise, planning, protocols, and training.

Hospital-Based Trauma System Considerations

Hospital challenges experienced in foreign and domestic bombings include:

- Difficulty in acquiring information from the scene
- Maldistribution of patients (e.g., two of 15 hospitals receiving approximately 60 percent of casualties from the scene in one large-scale event)
- A requirement for large numbers of hospital medical personnel to adequately treat the wounded
- The need to implement mass casualty contingency plans at every point of care (e.g., radiology postponing imaging an ankle sprain to rule out a fracture)
- Concern that the hospital may be a target
- Activation of Mass Transfusion Protocols, based on scope of injuries
- Activation of staff augmentation/call back plans, based on scope of injuries
- Initiation of patient movement/transfer plans, based on scope of injuries

Medical leaders of responses to bombings have noted that in many cases the majority of the injured and dead from large events present at the hospital closest to the scene. Patients able to leave the scene may forego EMS triage and present at hospitals before more severely injured patients arrive. The large influx of patients may exceed the hospital's capability to provide care, resulting in a "functional collapse" from inability to meet the demand spike. When this occurs, there is a compelling need to redistribute patients.

Distribution of patients among hospitals so that no one hospital exceeds its resources is a key principle in addressing medical surge capacity following terrorist bombings.

To address the large number of patients arriving at local facilities, local hospitals will need the swift assistance of incoming health care providers to assist with re-triage of the arriving casualties and the provision of appropriate services to patients. This influx will include additional doctors, nurses, medical specialists, such as blood bank technologists and respiratory therapists, mental health providers, and chaplains. In addition, there will likely be the need for law enforcement personnel to maintain order and security. In the hours immediately after the blast, these additional personnel will likely to come from surrounding communities and may require health care professionals from beyond the local area. While pre-event planning for cross-town (local) hospital credentialing and privileging of responding health care professionals can be arranged with relative ease, the issue of expeditious out-of-state credentialing and privileging of medical professionals responding to natural or man-made disasters can be more challenging.

Patient Movement/Transfer Considerations

As the patient load builds at local hospitals, some of the critically injured patients should be moved to other medical care facilities to optimize patient care. This will include movement to Level-1 trauma centers and other hospitals to better balance inpatient bed, operating room, intensive care unit, and rehabilitation bed utilization. Depending on the locality of the blast, this may include moving patients to other communities or across state lines. Long-distance transport of acutely injured patients will likely require aeromedical evacuation capabilities.

Scenario 3: Medium-Scale Terrorist/Insurgency Attack

Medium-scale attack using an IED with between 5 and 25 pounds net explosive weight. IEDs of this size frequently are placed in backpacks, suitcases, or buried and used to attack targets such as transportation infrastructure or specific locations to cause mass casualties with a potential of overwhelming the response and receiving infrastructure. This scenario includes suicide vest type devices that may be masked through clothing. Targets range from assassinations to mass casualties.

EXAMPLE: You are called to the scene of an explosion on a bus in your town center. A city bus full of passengers pulled into a crowded stop before exploding. You are the first arriving unit onto the scene...

Expected Injury Patterns

For those who survive this event, the injuries can include single and double amputees, extremity vascular injuries, penetrating foreign body thoraco-abdominal injuries, potential TBI and penetrating head trauma, neck trauma, and pulmonary contusions from closed space blasts.

Protective Equipment and Barriers

Secondary preventive measures include activities to prevent injuries once an explosion has occurred. Such measures may include barrier or structural walls that may protect or reduce injuries to bystanders and responders from blast and fragmentation injuries.[59] Secondary preventive measures also include use of ballistic protective equipment, although soft body armor and ceramic plate body armor may not protect against fragmentation or blast overpressure effects from IEDs. Most protective equipment is focused on ballistic protection and may have unproven or limited value for mitigating fragmentation or blast overpressure, particularly for devices with larger net explosive weights, such as vehicle bombs. For protective equipment and barriers to be effective, they must be implemented proactively; they are of little use when the explosive event is random and enacted on an unsuspecting, unprotected group of individuals. Ballistic protective equipment will also give some level of protection should an IED attack be combined with an active shooter event. Experience indicates attackers may plan to detonate secondary or subsequent IEDs that target first responders or receiving hospitals.

First responders should consider wearing some level of ballistic protective equipment. Considerations for first responder ballistic protective equipment should include what type of equipment is best suited for EMS and fire responders and when it should be worn (every shift, during times of high risk [e.g., on duty at a sports stadium], or just in response to IED events). It is critical that incident commanders base protective equipment and tactical movement guidance at the incident scene on a situational assessment of the IED risk, particularly when IEDs with significant net explosive weight are suspected or confirmed to be present. These types of IEDs, including vehicle bombs, may produce blast overpressure effects that would not be mitigated by typical protective equipment or available cover. A false sense of security among first responders could result if net explosive weight is not considered when determining protective equipment or tactical movement guidance to responders.

Protective Equipment Commonly Worn

Most law enforcement officers responding to the incident will be wearing Type II or IIIA bullet resistant vests, designed to stop bullets from most handguns, and shotgun pellets. Given the expected injuries, this level of protective equipment may not provide protection from blast overpressure and fragmentation, and extremities will be vulnerable. First responders other than law enforcement typically do not wear ballistic protective equipment. Civilians at public places will not be wearing any form of ballistic protective equipment.

Protective Equipment Risk Mitigation Considerations

The NIJ body armor standard specifies the ballistic threats that body armor must reliably protect against. This standard does not specify a requirement for ballistic resistant vests to

protect against fragmentation threats. The Type II or IIIA ballistic resistant vests that law enforcement officers are most commonly issued will likely not protect against fragmentation and blast overpressure effects from an IED threat. Use of Type IV body armor may increase the probability of protection against fragmentation and blast overpressure. However, further research and development is required to validate the performance of NIJ-approved body armor against fragmentation threats and to provide guidance on what level of protection should be worn to respond to this type of IED event.

Response and Incident Management Considerations

Maximize interoperability through existing MOUs/MOAs/SOPs, as well as through frequent exercises, planning, and training. These efforts will ultimately aid in reducing time from injury to treatment. During response, and while on the scene of the incident, use unified command with a mutual understanding of each responder's role (EMS, fire, and law enforcement). Strive to communicate on common frequencies and use standardized terminology. Ensure all responders (regardless of discipline — EMS, fire, law enforcement) are trained and equipped to provide early, aggressive hemorrhage control; use protective equipment (which includes ballistic vests, helmets, and eyewear); and use integrated response and incident management.

Medical Response System

An IED detonation has the potential of instantly producing hundreds of casualties (there were over 700 casualties after the Oklahoma City bombing) with injuries that range across the entire spectrum of severity. A system-wide medical response to this event should be well-coordinated, incorporating the lessons learned from the military (both system and individual patient care) and experiences from domestic and international bombings. Unlike the management of routine emergencies, the response to IED incidents will be extraordinary for the Nation's trauma and EMS systems.

System-wide efforts should include activities ranging from self-care, buddy-care, and bystander care to proper and effective prehospital triaging and patient transport to get the right patients to the appropriate medical facilities in a swift and orderly manner. The efforts include prehospital emergency medical services, ground ambulances, rotary and fixed wing aircraft patient transport, designated trauma centers, hospitals, and rehabilitation facilities.

Prehospital Emergency Medical Services Considerations

Patient-Based Considerations: The last decade of war has seen significant advances in the ability of prehospital care to impact the mortality of combat wounds. The ability to stop life-threatening bleeding from extremity wounds has been demonstrated to reduce the number of treatable exsanguination deaths.

As IEDs have become a common source of wounding in the wars in Iraq and Afghanistan, and as the use of IEDs in the United States (the Boston Marathon bombing on April 15, 2013) has become a reality, civilian adoption of some military clinical practices that are a significant departure from traditional prehospital care is appropriate:

- Aggressive hemorrhage control — including use of tourniquets and, where appropriate, hemostatic agents
- Aggressive airway management, including "sit up and lean forward" airway positioning
- Training all first responders in self-care, buddy care, and bystander care

System-Wide Implications

Experience from terrorist bombings occurring in other countries demonstrates common prehospital care system challenges, including multiple simultaneous attacks that cause an enormous number of casualties that exceed the available resources of EMS responders. The adoption of techniques that are suitable for use in self-care, buddycare, bystander care, and care delivered by first responders is essential to extend the range of persons providing immediate life-saving care.

EMS must rapidly and accurately triage casualties at the incident site and expeditiously transport those identified for "immediate care" into an appropriate hospital setting. It is imperative that pre-hospital triaging of wounded patients be as efficient and accurate as possible. Over-triage of patients over-taxes specialty centers that are designed to care for more significantly injured patients, while under-triaging of patients puts critically wounded patients into facilities that may not be able to provide the life-saving care needed. In addition to proper triage, care must be taken to regulate the transportation of casualties in order to direct victims to the hospital best suited for providing the necessary level of care for the type and severity of injuries they have sustained. Often the closest hospital is quickly overwhelmed by injured transported by ambulances, police cars, and privately owned vehicles, as well as the "walking wounded". Because the influx of patients to the nearest hospital is dictated by human behavior outside control of the system, the EMS system must recognize this likelihood and plan for redistribution of injured patients such that the closest hospital can return to maximum functionality as soon as possible. Incident managers should also anticipate the need to provide for safety and security with the arrival of injured persons' family members, the "psychologically shocked," and the media.

Hospital-Based Trauma System Considerations

Hospital challenges experienced in foreign and domestic bombings include:

- Difficulty in acquiring information from the scene
- Maldistribution of patients (e.g., two of 15 hospitals receiving approximately 60 percent of casualties from the scene in one large-scale event)
- A requirement for large numbers of hospital medical personnel to adequately treat the wounded
- The need to implement mass casualty contingency plans at every point of care (e.g., radiology postponing imaging an ankle sprain to rule out a fracture)
- Concern that the hospital may be a target
- Activation of Mass Transfusion Protocols, based on scope of injuries
- Activation of staff augmentation/call back plans, based on scope of injuries
- Initiation of patient movement/transfer plans, based on scope of injuries

Medical leaders of responses to bombings have noted that in many cases the majority of the injured and dead from large events present at the hospital closest to the scene. Patients able to leave the scene may forego EMS triage and present at hospitals before more severely injured patients arrive. The large influx of patients may exceed the hospital's capability to provide care, resulting in a "functional collapse" from inability to meet the demand spike. When this occurs, there is a compelling need to redistribute patients.

Distribution of patients among hospitals so that no one hospital exceeds its resources is a key principle in addressing medical surge capacity following bombing attacks that result in a significant number of casualties.

To address the large number of patients arriving at local facilities, local hospitals will need the swift assistance of incoming health care providers to assist with re-triage of the arriving casualties and the provision of appropriate services to patients. This influx will include additional doctors, nurses, medical specialists, such as blood bank technologists and respiratory therapists, mental health providers, and chaplains. In addition, there will likely be the need for law enforcement personnel to maintain order and security. In the hours immediately after the blast, these additional personnel will likely to come from surrounding communities and may require health care professionals from beyond the local area. While pre-event planning for cross-town (local) hospital credentialing and privileging of responding health care professionals can be arranged with relative ease, the issue of expeditious out-of-state credentialing and privileging of medical professionals responding to natural or man-made disasters can be more challenging.

Patient Movement/Transfer Considerations

As the patient load builds at local hospitals, some of the critically injured patients should be moved to other medical care facilities to optimize patient care. This will include movement to Level-1 trauma centers and other hospitals to better balance inpatient bed, operating room, intensive care unit, and rehabilitation bed utilization. Depending on the locality of the blast, this may include moving patients to other communities or across state lines. Long-distance transport of acutely injured patients will likely require aeromedical evacuation capabilities.

Scenario 4: Small Scale Terrorist/Insurgency Attack

Small-scale attack using an IED with less than 5 pounds net explosive weight. Assumed victim distance is 5 feet or less from center of the explosion. Use of high-energy explosives such as C-4 will cause smaller fragments traveling at higher velocity. Low-energy explosives, such as black powder filler in a pipe bomb, will generally result in larger fragments, which do not travel as far or fast. Oftentimes these small-scale attacks are targeted one-on-one events, and detonation occurs prior to first responder arrival.

EXAMPLE: You are called to the private residence for a reported explosion. One occupant of the house said his mother received and opened a package which detonated. There are two reported victims whose conditions are unknown. The caller was on the other side of the house when the explosion occurred...

Expected Injury Patterns

For those who survive this event, injuries can include digit and single amputees, soft tissue injuries, burns, ocular and tympanic injuries.

Protective Equipment and Barriers

Secondary preventive measures include activities to prevent injuries once an explosion has occurred. Such measures may include barrier or structural walls that may protect or reduce injuries to bystanders and responders from blast and fragmentation injuries.[60] Secondary preventive measures also include use of ballistic protective equipment, although soft body armor and ceramic plate body armor may not protect against fragmentation or blast overpressure effects from IEDs. Most protective equipment is focused on ballistic protection and may have unproven or limited value for mitigating fragmentation or blast overpressure, particularly for devices with larger net explosive weights, such as vehicle bombs. For protective equipment and barriers to be effective, they must be implemented proactively; they are of little use when the explosive event is random and enacted on an unsuspecting, unprotected group of individuals. Ballistic protective equipment will also give some level of protection should an IED attack be combined with an active shooter event. Experience indicates attackers may plan to detonate secondary or subsequent IEDs that target first responders or receiving hospitals.

First responders should consider wearing some level of ballistic protective equipment. Considerations for first responder ballistic protective equipment should include what type of equipment is best suited for EMS and fire responders and when it should be worn (every shift, during times of high risk [e.g., on duty at a sports stadium], or just in response to IED events). It is critical that incident commanders base protective equipment and tactical movement guidance at the incident scene on a situational assessment of the IED risk, particularly when IEDs with significant net explosive weight are suspected or confirmed to be present. These types of IEDs, including vehicle bombs, may produce blast overpressure effects that would not be mitigated by typical protective equipment or available cover. A false sense of security among first responders could result if net explosive weight is not considered when determining protective equipmentor tactical movement guidance to responders.

Protective Equipment Commonly Worn

Most law enforcement officers responding to the incident will be wearing Type II or IIIA bullet resistant vests, designed to stop bullets from most handguns, and shotgun pellets. Given the expected injuries, this level of protective equipment may not provide protection from blast overpressure and fragmentation, and extremities will be vulnerable. First responders other than law enforcement typically do not wear ballistic protective equipment. Civilians at public places will not be wearing any form of ballistic protective equipment.

Protective Equipment Risk Mitigation Considerations

The NIJ body armor standard specifies the ballistic threats that body armor must reliably protect against. This standard does not specify a requirement for ballistic resistant vests to

protect against fragmentation threats. The Type II or IIIA ballistic resistant vests that law enforcement officers are most commonly issued will likely not protect against fragmentation and blast overpressure effects from an IED threat. Use of Type IV body armor may increase the probability of protection against fragmentation and blast overpressure. However, further research and development is required to validate the performance of NIJ-approved body armor against fragmentation threats and to provide guidance on what level of protection should be worn to respond to this type of IED event.

Response and Incident Management Considerations

Maximize interoperability through existing MOUs/MOAs/SOPs, as well as through frequent exercises, planning, and training. These efforts will ultimately aid in reducing time from injury to treatment. During response, and while on the scene of the incident, use unified command with a mutual understanding of each responder's role (EMS, fire, and law enforcement). Strive to communicate on common frequencies and use standardized terminology. Ensure all responders (regardless of discipline — EMS, fire, law enforcement) are trained and equipped to provide early, aggressive hemorrhage control; use protective equipment (which includes ballistic vests, helmets, and eyewear); and use integrated response and incident management.

Medical Response System

Smaller explosives, such as with this scenario, present with response challenges and resource demands, but are not as taxing to the medical system as a larger IED. Response to this event would be well-coordinated, incorporating the lessons learned from the military (both system and individual patient care) and experiences from domestic and international bombings. Unlike the management of routine emergencies, the response to IED incidents will be extraordinary for the Nation's trauma and EMS systems.

System-wide efforts should include activities ranging from self-care, buddy-care, and bystander care to proper and effective prehospital triaging and patient transport to get the right patients to the appropriate medical facilities in a swift and orderly manner. The efforts include prehospital emergency medical services, ground ambulances, rotary and fixed wing aircraft patient transport, designated trauma centers, hospitals, and rehabilitation facilities.

Prehospital Emergency Medical Services Considerations

Patient-Based Considerations: The last decade of war has seen significant advances in the ability of prehospital care to impact the mortality of combat wounds. The ability to stop life-threatening bleeding from extremity wounds has been demonstrated to reduce the number of treatable exsanguination deaths.

As IEDs have become a common source of wounding in the wars in Iraq and Afghanistan, and as the use of IEDs in the United States (the Boston Marathon bombing on April 15, 2013) has become a reality, civilian adoption of some military clinical practices that are a significant departure from traditional prehospital care is appropriate:

- Aggressive hemorrhage control — including use of tourniquets and, where appropriate, hemostatic agents
- Aggressive airway management, including "sit up and lean forward" airway positioning
- Training all first responders in self-care, buddy care, and bystander care

System-Wide Implications

Experience from bombings occurring in other countries demonstrates common prehospital care system challenges, including multiple simultaneous attacks that cause an enormous number of casualties that exceed the available resources of EMS responders. The adoption of techniques that are suitable for use in self-care, buddy-care, bystander care, and care delivered by first responders is essential to extend the range of persons providing immediate life-saving care.

EMS must rapidly and accurately triage casualties at the incident site and expeditiously transport those identified for "immediate care" into an appropriate hospital setting. It is imperative that pre-hospital triaging of wounded patients be as efficient and accurate as possible. Over-triage of patients over-taxes specialty centers that are designed to care for more significantly injured patients, while under-triaging of patients puts critically wounded patients into facilities that may not be able to provide the life-saving care needed. In addition to proper triage, care must be taken to regulate the transportation of casualties in order to direct victims to the hospital best suited for providing the necessary level of care for the type and severity of injuries they have sustained. Often the closest hospital is quickly overwhelmed by injured transported by ambulances, police cars, and privately owned vehicles, as well as the "walking wounded". Because the influx of patients to the nearest hospital is dictated by human behavior outside control of the system, the EMS system must recognize this likelihood and plan for redistribution of injured patients such that the closest hospital can return to maximum functionality as soon as possible. Incident managers should also anticipate the need to provide for safety and security with the arrival of injured persons' family members, the "psychologically shocked," and the media.

EMS providers must also be cognizant of patients who appear otherwise well (uninjured), but may have traumatic brain injuries, tympanic membrane damage, and/or internal hollow organ damage due to the blast effects of the explosion. These considerations should be reinforced through exercise, planning, protocols, and training.

Hospital-Based Trauma System Considerations

Hospital challenges experienced in foreign and domestic bombings include:

- Difficulty in acquiring information from the scene
- Maldistribution of patients (e.g., two of 15 hospitals receiving approximately 60 percent of casualties from the scene in one large-scale event)
- A requirement for large numbers of hospital medical personnel to adequately treat the wounded
- The need to implement mass casualty contingency plans at every point of care (e.g., radiology postponing imaging an ankle sprain to rule out a fracture)
- Concern that the hospital may be a target
- Activation of Mass Transfusion Protocols, based on scope of injuries
- Activation of staff augmentation/call back plans, based on scope of injuries
- Initiation of patient movement/transfer plans, based on scope of injuries

Medical leaders of responses to bombings have noted that in many cases the majority of the injured and dead from large events present at the hospital closest to the scene. Patients able to leave the scene may forego EMS triage and present at hospitals before more severely injured patients arrive. The large influx of patients may exceed the hospital's capability to provide care, resulting in a "functional collapse" from inability to meet the demand spike. When this occurs, there is a compelling need to redistribute patients.

Distribution of patients among hospitals so that no one hospital exceeds its resources is a key principle in addressing medical surge capacity following bombing attacks that result in a significant number of casualties.

To address the large number of patients arriving at local facilities, local hospitals will need the swift assistance of incoming health care providers to assist with re-triage of the arriving casualties and the provision of appropriate services to patients. This influx will include additional doctors, nurses, medical specialists, such as blood bank technologists and respiratory therapists, mental health providers, and chaplains. In addition, there will likely be the need for law enforcement personnel to maintain order and security. In the hours immediately after the blast, these additional personnel will likely come from surrounding communities and may require health care professionals from beyond the local area. While pre-event planning for cross-town (local) hospital credentialing and privileging of responding health care professionals can be arranged with relative ease, the issue of expeditious out-of-state credentialing and privileging of medical professionals responding to natural or man-made disasters can been more has challenging.

Patient Movement/Transfer Considerations

As the patient load builds at local hospitals, some of the critically injured patients should be moved to other medical care facilities to optimize patient care. This will include movement to Level-1 trauma centers and other hospitals to better balance inpatient bed, operating room, intensive care unit, and rehabilitation bed utilization. Depending on the locality of the blast, this may include moving patients to other communities or across state lines. Long-distance transport of acutely injured patients will likely require aeromedical evacuation capabilities.

Scenario 5: Involuntary Suicide Bomber

This category of IED attack involves a subject who is forced to wear a suicide vest or carry an explosive device with between 5 and 25 pounds net explosive weight to attack targets such as critical infrastructure, mass gatherings or specific individuals. This scenario includes suicide vest type devices that may be masked through clothing. Targets range from assassinations to mass casualties. Assumed target victim distance is 5-10 feet from center of the explosion. Victims (targets and/or unwitting suicide bomber) will not likely have protective equipment.

EXAMPLE: You are called to a packed movie theater for a distressed subject. Upon arrival, you are met by a terrified looking individual standing in the theater lobby who has a locked suicide vest on his chest. He says that if the demands on the piece of paper he has are not met, the vest that is secured to his chest will be detonated by the men who wrote the letter. He starts approaching you and begs you to help him… The movie theater is packed and the patrons inside are unaware that the man has a suicide vest on him…

Expected Injury Patterns

For those who survive this event, single and double amputees, extremity vascular injuries, penetrating foreign body thoraco-abdominal injuries, potential TBI and penetrating head trauma, neck trauma, and pulmonary contusions from closed space blasts.

Protective Equipment and Barriers

Secondary preventive measures include activities to prevent injuries once an explosion has occurred. Such measures may include barrier or structural walls that may protect or reduce injuries to bystanders and responders from blast and fragmentation injuries.[61] Secondary preventive measures also include use of ballistic protective equipment, although soft body armor and ceramic plate body armor may not protect against fragmentation or blast overpressure effects from IEDs. Most protective equipment is focused on ballistic protection and may have unproven or limited value for mitigating fragmentation or blast overpressure, particularly for devices with larger net explosive weights, such as vehicle bombs. For protective equipment and barriers to be effective, they must be implemented proactively; they are of little use when the explosive event is random and enacted on an unsuspecting, unprotected group of individuals. Ballistic protective equipment will also give some level of protection should an IED attack be combined with an active shooter event. Experience indicates attackers may plan to detonate secondary or subsequent IEDs that target first responders or receiving hospitals.

First responders should consider wearing some level of ballistic protective equipment. Considerations for first responder ballistic protective equipment should include what type of equipment is best suited for EMS and fire responders and when it should be worn (every shift, during times of high risk [e.g., on duty at a sports stadium], or just in response to IED events). It is critical that incident commanders base protective equipment and tactical movement guidance at the incident scene on a situational assessment of the IED risk, particularly when IEDs with significant net explosive weight are suspected or confirmed to be present. These types of IEDs, including vehicle bombs, may produce blast overpressure effects that would not be mitigated by typical protective equipment or available cover. A false sense of security among first responders could result if net explosive weight is not considered when determining protective equipment or tactical movement guidance to responders.

Protective Equipment Commonly Worn

Most law enforcement officers responding to the incident will be wearing Type II or IIIA bullet resistant vests, designed to stop bullets from most handguns, and shotgun pellets. Given the expected injuries, this level of protective equipment may not provide protection from blast overpressure and fragmentation, and extremities will be vulnerable. First responders other than law enforcement typically do not wear ballistic protective equipment. Civilians at public places will not be wearing any form of ballistic protective equipment.

Protective Equipment Risk Mitigation Considerations

The NIJ body armor standard specifies the ballistic threats that body armor must reliably protect against. This standard does not specify a requirement for ballistic resistant vests to protect against fragmentation threats. The Type II or IIIA ballistic resistant vests that law enforcement officers are most commonly issued will likely not protect against fragmentation and blast overpressure effects from an IED threat. Use of Type IV body armor may increase the probability of protection against fragmentation and blast overpressure. However, further research and development is required to validate the performance of NIJ-approved body armor against fragmentation threats and to provide guidance on what level of protection should be worn to respond to this type of IED event.

Response and Incident Management Considerations

Maximize interoperability through existing MOUs/MOAs/SOPs, as well as through frequent exercises, planning, and training. These efforts will ultimately aid in reducing time from injury to treatment. During response, and while on the scene of the incident, use unified command with a mutual understanding of each responder's role (EMS, fire, and law enforcement). Strive to communicate on common frequencies and use standardized terminology. Ensure all responders (regardless of discipline — EMS, fire, law enforcement) are trained and equipped to provide early, aggressive hemorrhage control; use protective equipment (which includes ballistic vests, helmets, and eyewear); and use integrated response and incident management.

Medical Response System

An IED detonation has the potential of instantly producing hundreds of casualties (there were over 700 casualties after the Oklahoma City bombing) with injuries that range across the entire spectrum of severity. A system-wide medical response to this event should be well-coordinated, incorporating the lessons learned from the military (both system and individual patient care) and experiences from domestic and international bombings. Unlike the management of routine emergencies, the response to IED incidents will be extraordinary for the Nation's trauma and EMS systems.

System-wide efforts should include activities ranging from self-care, buddy-care, and bystander care to proper and effective prehospital triaging and patient transport to get the right patients to the appropriate medical facilities in a swift and orderly manner. The efforts include prehospital emergency medical services, ground ambulances, rotary and fixed wing aircraft patient transport, designated trauma centers, hospitals, and rehabilitation facilities.

Prehospital Emergency Medical Services Considerations

Patient-Based Considerations: The last decade of war has seen significant advances in the ability of prehospital care to impact the mortality of combat wounds. The ability to stop life-threatening bleeding from extremity wounds has been demonstrated to reduce the number of treatable exsanguination deaths.

As IEDs have become a common source of wounding in the wars in Iraq and Afghanistan, and as the use of IEDs in the United States (the Boston Marathon bombing on April 15, 2013) has become a reality, civilian adoption of some military clinical practices that are a significant departure from traditional prehospital care should be considered:

- Aggressive hemorrhage control — including use of tourniquets and, where appropriate, hemostatic agents
- Aggressive airway management, including "sit up and lean forward" airway positioning
- Training all first responders in self-care, buddy care, and bystander care

System-Wide Implications

Experience from bombing attacks occurring in other countries demonstrates common prehospital care system challenges, including multiple simultaneous attacks that cause an enormous number of casualties that exceed the available resources of EMS responders. The adoption of techniques that are suitable for use in self-care, buddycare, bystander care, and care delivered by first responders is essential to extend the depth of responders available to provide immediate life-saving care.

EMS must rapidly and accurately triage casualties at the incident site and expeditiously transport those identified for "immediate care" into an appropriate hospital setting. It is imperative that pre-hospital triaging of wounded patients be as efficient and accurate as possible. Over-triage of patients over-taxes specialty centers that are designed to care for more significantly injured patients, while under-triaging of patients puts critically wounded patients into facilities that may not be able to provide the life-saving care needed. In addition to proper triage, care must be taken to regulate the transportation of casualties in order to direct victims to the hospital best suited for providing the necessary level of care for the type and severity of injuries they have sustained. Often the closest hospital is quickly overwhelmed by injured transported by ambulances, police cars, and privately owned vehicles, as well as the "walking wounded". Because the influx of patients to the nearest hospital is dictated by human behavior outside control of the system, the EMS system must recognize this likelihood and plan for redistribution of injured patients such that the closest hospital can return to maximum functionality as soon as possible. Incident managers should also anticipate the need to provide for safety and security with the arrival of injured persons' family members, the "psychologically shocked," and the media.

EMS providers must also be cognizant of patients who appear otherwise well (uninjured), but may have traumatic brain injuries, tympanic membrane damage, and/or internal hollow organ damage due to the blast effects of the explosion. These considerations should be reinforced through exercise, planning, protocols, and training.

Hospital-Based Trauma System Considerations

Hospital challenges experienced in foreign and domestic terrorist bombings include:

- Difficulty in acquiring information from the scene
- Maldistribution of patients (e.g., two of 15 hospitals receiving approximately 60 percent of casualties from the scene in one large-scale event)
- A requirement for large numbers of hospital medical personnel to adequately treat the wounded
- The need to implement mass casualty contingency plans at every point of care (e.g., radiology postponing imaging an ankle sprain to rule out a fracture)
- Concern that the hospital may be a target
- Activation of Mass Transfusion Protocols, based on scope of injuries
- Activation of staff augmentation/call back plans, based on scope of injuries
- Initiation of patient movement/transfer plans, based on scope of injuries

Medical leaders of responses to bombings have noted that in many cases the majority of the injured and dead from large events present at the hospital closest to the scene. Patients able to leave the scene may forego EMS triage and present at hospitals before more severely injured patients arrive. The large influx of patients may exceed the hospital's capability to provide care, resulting in a "functional collapse" from inability to meet the demand spike. When this occurs, there is a compelling need to redistribute patients.

Distribution of patients among hospitals, so that no one hospital exceeds its resources, is a key principle in addressing medical surge capacity following bombing attacks that result in a significant number of casualties.

To address the large number of patients arriving at local facilities, local hospitals will need the swift assistance of incoming health care providers to assist with re-triage of the arriving casualties and the provision of appropriate services to patients. This influx will include additional doctors, nurses, medical specialists, such as blood bank technologists and respiratory therapists, mental health providers, and chaplains. In addition, there will likely be the need for law enforcement personnel to maintain order and security. In the hours immediately after the blast, these additional personnel will likely come from surrounding communities and may include health care professionals from beyond the local area. While pre-event planning for cross-town (local) hospital credentialing and privileging of responding health care professionals can be arranged with relative ease, the issue of expeditious out-of-state credentialing and privileging of medical professionals responding to natural or man-made disasters can be more challenging.

Scenario 6: Discovery/Recovery of Homemade Explosives (Not an Attack)

Many who seek explosives try to avoid detection by making their own explosives, often using ingredients and techniques found in on-line instructions. These "homemade" explosives are particularly dangerous, as they are made by inexperienced individuals outside of a formal manufacturing environment and without adequate quality control procedures. The homemade manufacture of primary explosives such as Hexamethlene Triperoxide Diamine (HMTD), Triacetone-Triperoxide (TATP), and Lead Azide are of greatest concern due to their unpredictable nature as well as sensitivity to heat, friction, and shock. First responders including fire/ HAZMAT, paramedics, and law enforcement are particularly vulnerable as clandestine labs encountered may look similar to illicit drug labs. In this type of scenario, the victim — either manufacturer or first responder — is often in direct contact with the explosive materials.

EXAMPLE: You are on the scene of a basement fire where firefighters have removed a victim who is unresponsive, but alive. The victim has blast injuries and amputation of his right hand and several fingers from his left hand. The firefighters indicate that the fire is contained, but that there are several containers of unknown materials adjacent to where the fire and reported explosion occurred...

Expected Injury Patterns

For those who survive this event, injuries are often burns and/or traumatic amputation of fingers or limbs, soft tissue injuries, ocular injuries, and ruptured eardrums, depending on the quantity and type of homemade explosive encountered.

Protective Equipment and Barriers

In the absence of further patients requiring care, the scene should be isolated, and only entered by first responders with the appropriate level of protective equipment. A determination will need to be made on scene as to whether flash, hazmat or EOD (bomb suit) protection is indicated. It is critical that incident commanders base protective equipment and tactical movement guidance at the incident scene on a situation assessment of the IED risk, particularly when IEDs with significant net explosive weight are suspected or confirmed to be present. These types of IEDs, including vehicle bombs, may produce overpressure blast effects regardless of fragmentation that would not be mitigated by typical protective equipment or available cover. A false sense of security among first responders could result if net explosive weight is not considered when determining protective equipment or tactical movement guidance to responders.

Protective Equipment Commonly Worn

Law enforcement officers will wear Type II or IIIA bullet resistant vests, designed to stop bullets from most handguns, shotgun pellets, and blunt shrapnel. First responders other than law enforcement typically do not wear ballistic protective equipment. Fire responders wear fire resistant jackets/pants with helmets, which provide thermal protection. Explosive Ordnance Disposal/bomb technicians wear either a full bomb suit or, in some circumstances, less restrictive protective equipment to improve maneuverability.

Response and Incident Management Considerations

Maximize interoperability through existing MOUs/MOAs/SOPs, as well as through frequent exercises, planning, and training. These efforts will ultimately aid in reducing time from injury to treatment. During response, and while on the scene of the incident, use unified command with a mutual understanding of each responder's role (EMS, fire, and law enforcement). Strive to communicate on common frequencies and use standardized terminology. Ensure all responders (regardless of discipline — EMS, fire, law enforcement) are trained and equipped to provide early, aggressive hemorrhage control; use protective equipment (which includes ballistic vests, helmets, and eyewear); and use integrated response and incident management.

Prehospital Emergency Medical Services Considerations

Patient-Based Considerations: The last decade of war has seen significant advances in the ability of prehospital care to impact the mortality of combat wounds. The ability to stop life-threatening bleeding from extremity wounds has been demonstrated to reduce the number of treatable exsanguination deaths.

As IEDs have become a common source of wounding in the wars in Iraq and Afghanistan, and as the use of IEDs in the United States (the Boston Marathon bombing on April 15, 2013) has become a reality, civilian adoption of some military clinical practices that are a significant departure from traditional prehospital care should be considered:

- Aggressive hemorrhage control — including use of tourniquets and, where appropriate, hemostatic agents
- Aggressive airway management, including "sit up and lean forward" airway positioning
- Training all first responders in self-care, buddy care, and bystander care
- In this scenario, the need for decontamination of patients and responders must be considered

Scenario 7: Active Shooter with Access Denial to First Responders

Two shooters attack an indoor public building using firearms , and disperse potentially lethal chemicals in an effort to deny first responder access to the scene. The shooters placed buckets of chemicals adjacent to two primary entry/exit points, creating toxic clouds to block first responders, and then opened fire with semiautomatic weapons, handguns, and shotguns within the center of the building, where approximately 300 people were gathered.

EXAMPLE: You are called to the scene of an indoor shopping mall on a busy day. As the first arriving unit, you see people running from the facility and several victims on the ground immediately outside the exit door in front of you. Several of the people who escaped are in apparent distress and are having trouble breathing. There are three victims who are bleeding and are being cared for by bystanders. You also see a white cloud coming out of the door and hear gunfire from what appears to be several different sources...

Expected Injury Patterns

Multiple gunshot wounds from various caliber weapons; wide-spread casualties from gunshot wounds, chemical exposure, and care delay; and non-firearm-related injuries associated with attempts to escape (lacerations, fractures). The chemicals produce hazardous to potentially lethal effects and a barrier that will significantly delay access by all first responders not prepared to enter into a hazardous materials environment. Traditional HAZ/MAT response results in delays that will promote wide-spread hemorrhage.

Protective Equipment and Barriers

First responders should consider wearing protective equipment to mitigate ballistic, respiratory and mucous membrane, and dermal hazards. Utilizing available barriers or structural walls can also provide protective cover and/or concealment for first responders within the shooter's field of fire. Preventive measures also include use of ballistic protective equipment, although soft body armor and ceramic plate body armor may not protect against fragmentation or blast overpressure effects from IEDs. Most protective equipment is focused on ballistic protection and may have unproven or limited value for mitigating fragmentation or blast overpressure, particularly for devices with larger net explosive weights, such as vehicle bombs. For protective equipment and barriers to be effective, they must be implemented proactively; they are of little use when the explosive event is random and enacted on an unsuspecting, unprotected group of individuals. Ballistic protective equipment will also give some level of protection should an IED attack be combined with an active shooter event. Experience indicates attackers may plan to detonate secondary or subsequent IEDs that target first responders or receiving hospitals.

Protective Equipment Commonly Worn

Most law enforcement officers responding to the incident will be wearing Type II or IIIA bullet resistant vests, designed to stop bullets from most handguns, and shotgun pellets. First responders other than law enforcement typically do not wear ballistic protective equipment. Civilians at public places such will not be wearing any form of ballistic protective equipment.

Protective Equipment Risk Mitigation Considerations

Responders should utilize the highest level of protective equipment available to them — ideally Type IV ballistic vests and helmets when responding to active shooter incidents. The NIJ body armor standard specifies ballistic threats that body armor must reliably protect against.[62][63] Protection against common industrial hazardous chemicals — with a focus on respiratory, eyes, mucous membranes and skin protection — can be provided by first responder turnout gear, SCBA (SelfContained Breathing Apparatus), gas masks, and Victim Rescue Units or Tyvek® suits.

Response and Incident Management Considerations

Maximize interoperability through existing MOUs/MOAs/SOPs, as well as through frequent exercises, planning, and training. These efforts will ultimately aid in reducing time from injury to treatment. During response, and while on the scene of the incident, use unified command with a mutual understanding of each responder's role (EMS, fire, and law enforcement). Strive to communicate on common frequencies and use standardized terminology. Ensure all responders (regardless of discipline — EMS, fire, law enforcement) are trained and equipped to provide early, aggressive hemorrhage control; use protective equipment (which includes ballistic vests, helmets, and eyewear); and use integrated response and incident management.

Medical Response System

An active shooter incident complicated by a hazardous materials release has the potential to produce large numbers of casualties with injuries that range across the entire spectrum of severity. In addition to mass casualty trauma care, high consideration of decontamination requirements must be taken. A system-wide medical response to this event should be well-coordinated, incorporating the lessons learned from the military (both system and individual patient care) and experiences from domestic and international incidents. Unlike the management of routine emergencies, the response to active shooter incidents will be extraordinary for the Nation's trauma and EMS systems.

System-wide efforts should include activities ranging from self-care, buddy-care, and bystander care to proper and effective prehospital triaging and patient transport to get the right patients to the appropriate medical facilities in a swift and orderly manner. The efforts include prehospital emergency medical services, ground ambulances, rotary and fixed wing aircraft patient transport, designated trauma centers, hospitals, and rehabilitation facilities.

Prehospital Emergency Medical Services Considerations

Patient-Based Considerations: The last decade of war has seen significant advances in the ability of prehospital care to impact the mortality of combat wounds. The ability to stop life-threatening bleeding from extremity wounds has been demonstrated to reduce the number of treatable exsanguination deaths.

As active shooter incidents have become a common source of wounding in the United States, civilian adoption of some military clinical practices that are a significant departure from traditional prehospital care should be considered:

- Aggressive hemorrhage control — including use of tourniquets and, where appropriate, hemostatic agents
- Aggressive airway management, including "sit up and lean forward" airway positioning
- Training all first responders in self-care, buddy care, and bystander care
- In this scenario, the need for decontamination of patients and responders must be considered

System-Wide Implications

Experience from attacks (active shooter incidents) occurring in other countries demonstrates common prehospital care system challenges, including multiple simultaneous attacks that cause an enormous number of casualties that exceed the available resources of EMS responders. The adoption of techniques that are suitable for use in self-care, buddy-care, bystander care, and care delivered by first responders is essential to extend the depth of responders available to provide immediate life-saving care.

EMS must rapidly and accurately triage casualties at the incident site and expeditiously transport those identified for "immediate care" into an appropriate hospital setting. It is imperative that pre-hospital triaging of wounded patients be as efficient and accurate as possible. Over-triage of patients over-taxes specialty centers that are designed to care for more significantly injured patients, while under-triaging of patients puts critically wounded patients into facilities that may not be able to provide the life-saving care needed. In addition to proper triage, care must be taken to regulate the transportation of casualties in order to direct victims to the hospital best suited for providing the necessary level of care for the type and severity of injuries they have sustained. Often the closest hospital is quickly overwhelmed by injured transported by ambulances, police cars, and privately owned vehicles, as well as the "walking wounded". Because the influx of patients to the nearest hospital is dictated by human behavior outside control of the system, the EMS system must recognize this likelihood and plan for redistribution of injured patients such that the closest hospital can return to maximum functionality as soon as possible. Incident managers should also anticipate the need to provide for safety and security with the arrival of injured persons' family members, the "psychologically shocked," and the media.

From a law enforcement perspective, the following should be considered:

- Law enforcement units should be trained in active shooter response, to include deployment of a contact team and a follow-on rescue team, depending on local resources and system configuration.
- All first responders (EMS, fire, and law enforcement) should be trained and practiced to work together in active shooter scenarios.
- Active shooter first response should focus on traditional Care Under Fire injuries with immediate "Extraction" from the site of the attack as a priority. All casualties should be directed or moved to a "Safe Point" (a secure location near the attack) by extraction teams where the casualties will be retriaged and treated for transfer.
- Interoperability between EMS, fire and law enforcement personnel must be exercised and an understanding of the responsibilities and actions of all parties is essential. This is achieved through mutual trainings, well-developed policies, and tabletop exercises.
- State and local officials should promote CERTs to deliver civilian training in conjunction with nongovernmental organizations.

Experience from active shooter incidents and bombing attacks demonstrates common prehospital care system challenges, including multiple simultaneous attacks that cause an enormous number of casualties that exceed the available resources of EMS responders. The adoption of techniques that are suitable for use in self-care, buddycare, bystander care, and care delivered by first responders is essential to extend the range of persons providing immediate life-saving care. First responders should develop plans for working on "contaminated casualties".

EMS providers must also be cognizant of patients who appear otherwise well (uninjured), but may have hidden injuries and exposure to hazardous materials. These considerations should be reinforced through exercise, planning, protocols, and training.

Hospital-Based Trauma System Considerations

Hospital challenges experienced in foreign and domestic active shooter incidents include:

- Difficulty in acquiring information from the scene
- Maldistribution of patients (e.g., two of 15 hospitals receiving approximately 60 percent of casualties from the scene in one large-scale event)
- A requirement for large numbers of hospital medical personnel to adequately treat the wounded
- The need to implement mass casualty contingency plans at every point of care (e.g., radiology postponing imaging an ankle sprain to rule out a fracture)
- Concern that the hospital may be a target
- Activation of Mass Transfusion Protocols, based on scope of injuries
- Activation of staff augmentation/call back plans, based on scope of injuries
- Initiation of patient movement/transfer plans, based on scope of injuries

Medical leaders of responses to attacks have noted that in many cases the majority of the injured and dead from large events present at the hospital closest to the scene. Patients able to leave the scene may forego EMS triage and present at hospitals before more severely injured patients arrive. The large influx of patients may exceed the hospital's capability to provide care, resulting in a "functional collapse" from inability to meet the demand spike. When this occurs, there is a compelling need to redistribute patients.

Distribution of patients among hospitals, so that no one hospital exceeds its resources, is a key principle in addressing medical surge capacity following bombing attacks that result in a significant number of casualties.

To address the large number of patients arriving at local facilities, local hospitals will need the swift assistance of incoming health care providers to assist with re-triage of the arriving casualties and the provision of appropriate services to patients. This influx will include additional doctors, nurses, medical specialists, such as blood bank technologists and respiratory therapists, mental health providers, and chaplains. In addition, there will likely be the need for law enforcement personnel to maintain order and security. In the hours immediately after the in-cident, these additional personnel will likely come from surrounding communities and may include health care professionals from beyond the local area. While pre-event planning for cross-town (local) hospital credentialing and privileging of responding health care professionals can be arranged with relative ease, the issue of expedi-tious out-of-state credentialing and privileging of medical professionals responding to natural or man-made disasters can be more challenging.

Patient Movement/Transfer Considerations

As the patient load builds at local hospitals, some of the critically injured patients should be moved to other medical care facilities to optimize patient care. This will include movement to Level-1 trauma centers and other hospitals to better balance inpatient bed, operating room, intensive care unit, and rehabilitation bed utilization. Depending on the locality of the incident, this may include moving patients to other communities or across state lines. Long-distance transport of acutely injured patients will likely require aeromedical evacuation capabilities.

Scenario 8: Active Shooter in a Public Commercial Facility

A lone gunman enters a public commercial facility and starts methodically moving through the building, shooting everyone he encounters. The gunman is armed with two handguns, a shotgun and a semi-automatic rifle. According to a witness who escaped, there are approximately 60 individuals in the facility. The gunmen used bike locks to immobilize exit doors.

EXAMPLE: You are the first arriving unit to a supermarket where terrified people are running from side doors and are seeking cover in the parking lot and surrounding area. You see four people with obvious gunshot wounds, one of whom is obviously deceased. You hear continued gunfire from your location...

Expected Injury Patterns

Multiple gunshot wounds from various caliber weapons, wide-spread casualties from gunshot wounds and care delay, and non-firearm-related injuries associated with attempts to escape (lacerations, fractures).

Protective Equipment and Barriers

First responders should consider wearing some level of ballistic protective equipment. Utilizing available barriers or structural walls can also provide protective cover and/or concealment for first responders within the shooter's field of fire. Preventive measures also include use of ballistic protective equipment, although soft body armor and ceramic plate body armor may not protect against fragmentation or blast overpressure effects from IEDs. Most protective equipment is focused on ballistic protection and may have unproven or limited value for mitigating fragmentation or blast overpressure, particularly for devices with larger net explosive weights, such as vehicle bombs. For protective equipment and barriers to be effective, they must be implemented proactively; they are of little use when the explosive event is random and enacted on an unsuspecting, unprotected group of individuals. Ballistic protective equipment will also give some level of protection should an IED attack be combined with an active shooter event. Experience indicates attackers may plan to detonate secondary or subsequent IEDs that target first responders or receiving hospitals.

Protective Equipment Commonly Worn

Most law enforcement officers responding to the incident will be wearing Type II or IIIA bullet resistant vests, designed to stop bullets from most handguns, and shotgun pellets. First responders other than law enforcement typically do not wear ballistic protective equipment. Civilians at public places such will not be wearing any form of ballistic protective equipment.

Protective Equipment Risk Mitigation Considerations

Responders should utilize the highest level of protective equipment available to them — ideally Type IV ballistic vests and helmets when responding to active shooter incidents. The NIJ body armor standard specifies ballistic threats that body armor must reliably protect against.[44][45]

Response and Incident Management Considerations

Maximize interoperability through existing MOUs/MOAs/SOPs, as well as through frequent exercises, planning, and training. These efforts will ultimately aid in reducing time from injury to treatment. During response, and while on the scene of the incident, use unified command with a mutual understanding of each responder's role (EMS, fire, and law enforcement). Strive to communicate on common frequencies and use standardized terminology. Ensure all responders (regardless of discipline — EMS, fire, law enforcement) are trained and equipped to provide early, aggressive hemorrhage control; use protective equipment (which includes ballistic vests, helmets, and eyewear); and use integrated response and incident management.

Medical Response System

A system-wide medical response to this event should be well-coordinated, incorporating the lessons learned from the military (both system and individual patient care) and experiences from domestic and international active shooter incidents. Unlike the management of routine emergencies, the response to active shooter incidents will be extraordinary for the Nation's trauma and EMS systems.

System-wide efforts should include activities ranging from self-care, buddy-care, and bystander care to proper and effective prehospital triaging and patient transport to get the right patients to the appropriate medical facilities in a swift and orderly manner. The efforts include prehospital emergency medical services, ground ambulances, rotary and fixed wing aircraft patient transport, designated trauma centers, hospitals, and rehabilitation facilities.

Prehospital Emergency Medical Services Considerations

Patient-Based Considerations: The last decade of war has seen significant advances in the ability of prehospital care to impact the mortality of combat wounds. The ability to stop life-threatening bleeding from extremity wounds has been demonstrated to reduce the number of treatable exsanguination deaths.

As active shooter incidents have become a common source of wounding in the United States, civilian adoption of some military clinical practices that are a significant departure from traditional prehospital care should be considered:

- Aggressive hemorrhage control — including use of tourniquets and, where appropriate, hemostatic agents
- Aggressive airway management, including "sit up and lean forward" airway positioning
- Training all first responders in self-care, buddy care, and bystander care

System-Wide Implications

Experience from terrorist attacks (active shooter incidents) occurring in other countries demonstrates common prehospital care system challenges, including multiple simultaneous attacks that cause an enormous number of casualties that exceed the available resources of EMS responders. The adoption of techniques that are suitable for use in self-care, buddy-care, bystander care, and care delivered by first responders is essential to extend the depth of responders available to provide immediate life-saving care.

EMS must rapidly and accurately triage casualties at the incident site and expeditiously transport those identified for "immediate care" into an appropriate hospital setting. It is imperative that pre-hospital triaging of wounded patients be as efficient and accurate as possible. Over-triage of patients over-taxes specialty centers that are designed to care for more significantly injured patients, while under-triaging of patients puts critically wounded patients into facilities that may not be able to provide the life-saving care needed. In addition to proper triage, care must be taken to regulate the transportation of casualties in order to direct victims to the hospital best suited for providing the necessary level of care for the type and severity of injuries they have sustained. Often the closest hospital is quickly overwhelmed by injured transported by ambulances, police cars, and privately owned vehicles, as well as the "walking wounded". Because the influx of patients to the nearest hospital is dictated by human behavior outside control of the system, the EMS system must recognize this likelihood and plan for redistribution of injured patients such that the closest hospital can return to maximum functionality as soon as possible. Incident managers should also anticipate the need to provide for safety and security with the arrival of injured persons' family members, the "psychologically shocked," and the media.

From a law enforcement perspective, the following should be considered:

- Law enforcement units should be trained in active shooter response, to include deployment of a contact team and a follow-on rescue team, depending on local resources and system configuration.
- All first responders (EMS, fire, and law enforcement) should be trained and practiced to work together in active shooter scenarios.
- Active shooter first response should focus on traditional Care Under Fire injuries with immediate "Extraction" from the site of the attack as a priority. All casualties should

be directed or moved to a "Safe Point" (a secure location near the attack) by extraction teams where the casualties will be retriaged and treated for transfer.
- Interoperability between EMS, fire and law enforcement personnel must be exercised, and an understanding of the responsibilities and actions of all parties is essential. This is achieved through mutual trainings, well-developed policies, and tabletop exercises.
- State and local officials should promote CERTs to deliver civilian training in conjunction with nongovernmental organizations.

Experience from active shooter incidents and bombing attacks demonstrates common prehospital care system challenges, including multiple simultaneous attacks that cause an enormous number of casualties that exceed the available resources of EMS responders. The adoption of techniques that are suitable for use in self-care, buddycare, bystander care, and care delivered by first responders is essential to extend the range of persons providing immediate life-saving care.

Hospital-Based Trauma System Considerations

Hospital challenges experienced in foreign and domestic active shooter incidents include:

- Difficulty in acquiring information from the scene
- Maldistribution of patients (e.g., two of 15 hospitals receiving approximately 60 percent of casualties from the scene in one large-scale event)
- A requirement for large numbers of hospital medical personnel to adequately treat the wounded
- The need to implement mass casualty contingency plans at every point of care (e.g., radiology postponing imaging an ankle sprain to rule out a fracture)
- Concern that the hospital may be a target
- Activation of Mass Transfusion Protocols, based on scope of injuries
- Activation of staff augmentation/call back plans, based on scope of injuries
- Initiation of patient movement/transfer plans, based on scope of injuries

Medical leaders of responses to attacks have noted that in many cases the majority of the injured and dead from large events present at the hospital closest to the scene. Patients able to leave the scene may forego EMS triage and present at hospitals before more severely injured patients arrive. The large influx of patients may exceed the hospital's capability to provide care, resulting in a "functional collapse" from inability to meet the demand spike. When this occurs, there is a compelling need to redistribute patients.

Distribution of patients among hospitals, so that no one hospital exceeds its resources, is a key principle in addressing medical surge capacity following bombing attacks that result in a significant number of casualties.

To address the large number of patients arriving at local facilities, local hospitals will need the swift assistance of incoming health care providers to assist with re-triage of the arriving casualties and the provision of appropriate services to patients. This influx will include additional doctors, nurses, medical specialists, such as blood bank technologists and respiratory therapists, mental health providers, and chaplains. In addition, there will likely be the need for law enforcement personnel to maintain order and security. In the hours immediately after the blast, these additional personnel will likely come from surrounding communities and may include health care professionals from beyond the local area. While pre-event planning for cross-town (local) hospital credentialing and privileging of responding health care professionals can be arranged with relative ease, the issue of expeditious out-of-state credentialing and privileging of medical professionals responding to natural or man-made disasters can be more challenging.

Patient Movement/Transfer Considerations

As the patient load builds at local hospitals, some of the critically injured patients should be moved to other medical care facilities to optimize patient care. This will include movement to Level-1 trauma centers and other hospitals to better balance inpatient bed, operating room, intensive care unit, and rehabilitation bed utilization. Depending on the locality of the incident, this may include moving patients to other communities or across state lines. Long-distance transport of acutely injured patients will likely require aeromedical evacuation capabilities.

Distribution of patients among hospitals, so that no one hospital exceeds its resources, is a key principle in addressing medical surge capacity following bombing attacks that result in a significant number of casualties.

To address the large number of patients arriving at local facilities, local hospitals will need the swift assistance of incoming health care providers to assist with re-triage of the arriving casualties and the provision of appropriate services to patients. This influx will include additional doctors, nurses, medical specialists, such as blood bank technologists and respiratory therapists, mental health providers, and chaplains. In addition, there will likely be the need for law enforcement personnel to maintain order and security. In the hours immediately after the incident, these additional personnel will likely come from surrounding communities and may include health care professionals from beyond the local area. While pre-event planning for cross-town (local) hospital credentialing and privileging of responding health care professionals can be arranged with relative ease, the issue of expeditious out-of-state credentialing and privileging of medical professionals responding to natural or man-made disasters can be more challenging.

Scenario 9: Active Shooter in an Open, Outdoor, Unbounded Location

A single gunman enters a building and takes and elevated position, overlooking a crowded courtyard. The gunman is armed with handguns and a scoped hunting rifle. There are approximately 165 people currently in the courtyard as the gunman commences firing into the crowd.

EXAMPLE: You are the first arriving unit to a reported active shooter incident at an open courtyard at an academic institution. As you approach, there are many people running away from the facility. You notice several injured people with bystanders rendering care, as well as several victims who are obviously deceased. The crowd egressing is panic-stricken and seeking cover as you hear continued gunfire.

Expected Injury Patterns

Multiple gunshot wounds from mostly high-caliber weapons, wide-spread casualties from gunshot wounds and care delay, and non-firearm-related injuries associated with attempts to escape (lacerations, fractures).

Protective Equipment and Barriers

First responders should consider wearing protective equipment to mitigate ballistic, respiratory and mucous membrane, and dermal hazards. Utilizing available barriers or structural walls can also provide protective cover and/or concealment for first responders within the shooter's field of fire. Ballistic protective equipment includes soft body armor and ceramic plate body armor, and may also provide some level of protection should the active shooter event be combined with a secondary or subsequent IED attack. Experience indicates attackers may plan to detonate secondary or subsequent IEDs that target first responders or receiving hospitals.

Considerations for first responder ballistic protective equipment should include what type of equipment is best suited for EMS responders and when it should be worn (every shift, during times of high risk [e.g., on duty at a sports stadium], or just in response to IED events).

Protective Equipment Commonly Worn

Most law enforcement officers responding to the incident will be wearing Type II or IIIA bullet resistant vests, designed to stop bullets from most handguns, and shotgun pellets. First responders other than law enforcement typically do not wear ballistic protective equipment. Civilians at public places such will not be wearing any form of ballistic protective equipment.

Protective Equipment Risk Mitigation Considerations

Responders should utilize the highest level of protective equipment available to them — ideally Type IV ballistic vests and helmets. The NIJ body armor standard specifies ballistic threats that body armor must reliably protect against.[64][65]

Response and Incident Management Considerations

Maximize interoperability to the extent possible (through prior MOUs/MOAs/SOPs) to reduce time from injury to treatment. Strive to communicate on common frequencies and use standardized terminology. Ensure all responders (regardless of discipline — EMS, fire, law enforcement) are trained and equipped to provide early, aggressive hemorrhage control; use body armor; use a more integrated response and incident management.

Flexibility is key in how effectively aid is delivered to the injured — a single solution may not work best in all scenarios (e.g., law enforcement brings the injured out to safety, law enforcement escorts EMS/fire into transitional zones, law enforcement provides care).

Medical Response System

System-wide efforts should include activities ranging from self-care, buddy-care, and bystander care to regional and multi-state trauma responses. The efforts include prehospital emergency medical services, ground ambulances, rotary and fixed wing aircraft patient transport, designated trauma centers, hospitals, and rehabilitation facilities. Unlike the management of routine emergencies, the response to active shooter incidents will be extraordinary for the Nation's trauma and EMS systems.

Prehospital Emergency Medical Services Considerations

Patient-Based Considerations: The last decade of war has seen significant advances in the ability of prehospital care to impact the mortality of combat wounds. The ability to stop life-threatening bleeding from extremity wounds has been demonstrated to reduce the number of treatable exsanguination deaths. Civilian adoption of some military clinical practices that are a significant departure from traditional prehospital care is appropriate:

- Aggressive hemorrhage control — including use of tourniquets and, where appropriate, hemostatic agents
- Aggressive airway management, including "sit up and lean forward" airway positioning
- Training all first responders in self-care, buddy care, and bystander care

System-Wide Implications

Experience from terrorist attacks (active shooter incidents) occurring in other countries demonstrates common prehospital care system challenges, including multiple simultaneous attacks that cause an enormous number of casualties that exceed the available resources of EMS responders. The adoption of techniques that are suitable for use in self-care, buddy-care, bystander care, and care delivered by first responders is essential to extend the depth of responders available to provide immediate life-saving care.

EMS must rapidly and accurately triage casualties at the incident site and expeditiously transport those identified for "immediate care" into an appropriate hospital setting. It is imperative that pre-hospital triaging of wounded patients be as efficient and accurate as possible. Over-triage of patients over-taxes specialty centers that are designed to care for more significantly injured patients, while under-triaging of patients puts critically wounded patients into facilities that may not be able to provide the life-saving care needed. In addition to proper triage, care must be taken to regulate the transportation of casualties in order to direct victims to the hospital best suited for providing the necessary level of care for the type and severity of injuries they have sustained. Often the closest hospital is quickly overwhelmed by injured transported by ambulances, police cars, and privately owned vehicles, as well as the "walking wounded". Because the influx of patients to the nearest hospital is dictated by human behavior outside control of the system, the EMS system must recognize this likelihood and plan for redistribution of injured patients such that the closest hospital can return to maximum functionality as soon as possible. Incident managers should also anticipate the need to provide for safety and security with the arrival of injured persons' family members, the "psychologically shocked," and the media.

From a law enforcement perspective, the following should be considered:

- Law enforcement units should be trained in active shooter response, to include deployment of a contact team and a follow-on rescue team, depending on local resources and system configuration.
- All first responders (EMS, fire, and law enforcement) should be trained and practiced to work together in active shooter scenarios.
- Active shooter first response should focus on traditional Care Under Fire injuries with immediate "Extraction" from the site of the attack as a priority. All casualties should be directed or moved to a "Safe Point" (a secure location near the attack) by extraction teams where the casualties will be retriaged and treated for transfer.
- Interoperability between EMS, fire, and law enforcement personnel must be exercised, and an understanding of the responsibilities and actions of all parties is essential. This is achieved through mutual trainings, well-developed policies, and tabletop exercises.

State and local officials should promote CERTs to deliver civilian training in conjunction with non-governmental organizations.

Hospital-Based Trauma System Considerations

Hospital challenges experienced in foreign and domestic active shooter incidents include:

- Difficulty in acquiring information from the scene
- Maldistribution of patients (e.g., two of 15 hospitals receiving approximately 60 percent of casualties from the scene in one large-scale event)
- A requirement for large numbers of hospital medical personnel to adequately treat the wounded
- The need to implement mass casualty contingency plans at every point of care (e.g., radiology postponing imaging an ankle sprain to rule out a fracture)
- Concern that the hospital may be a target
- Activation of Mass Transfusion Protocols, based on scope of injuries
- Activation of staff augmentation/call back plans, based on scope of injuries
- Initiation of patient movement/transfer plans, based on scope of injuries

Medical leaders of responses to attacks have noted that in many cases the majority of the injured and dead from large events present at the hospital closest to the scene. Patients able to leave the scene may forego EMS triage and present at hospitals before more severely injured patients arrive. The large influx of patients may exceed the hospital's capability to provide care, resulting in a "functional collapse" from inability to meet the demand spike. When this occurs, there is a compelling need to redistribute patients.

Distribution of patients among hospitals, so that no one hospital exceeds its resources, is a key principle in addressing medical surge capacity following bombing attacks that result in a significant number of casualties.

To address the large number of patients arriving at local facilities, local hospitals will need the swift assistance of incoming health care providers to assist with re-triage of the arriving casualties and the provision of appropriate services to patients. This influx will include additional doctors, nurses, medical specialists, such as blood bank technologists and respiratory therapists, mental health providers, and chaplains. In addition, there will likely be the need for law enforcement personnel to maintain order and security. In the hours immediately after the blast, these additional personnel will likely come from surrounding communities and may include health care professionals from beyond the local area. While pre-event planning for cross-town (local) hospital credentialing and privileging of responding health care professionals can be arranged with relative ease, the issue of expeditious out-of-state credentialing and privileging of medical professionals responding to natural or manmade disasters can be more challenging.

Patient Movement/Transfer Considerations

As the patient load builds at local hospitals, some of the critically injured patients should be moved to other medical care facilities to optimize patient care. This will include movement to Level-1 trauma centers and other hospitals to better balance inpatient bed, operating room, intensive care unit, and rehabilitation bed utilization. Depending on the locality of the incident, this may include moving patients to other communities or across state lines. Long-distance transport of acutely injured patients will likely require aeromedical evacuation capabilities.

Scenario 10: Active Shooter in a Public Sports Complex

Three gunmen enter a sporting complex that is filled with spectators. One gunman is located at an exit gate and the other two are positioned in the stadium and they all commence firing randomly at spectators. They are armed with handguns, shotguns and semi-automatic rifles. The facility currently has approximately 24,000 people in attendance.

EXAMPLE: You are the first arriving unit to a reported active shooter incident at a sport complex. As you approach, there are many people running away from the facility. Several security personnel and law enforcement officers working the event are seen on the outside perimeter of the complex...

Expected Injury Patterns

Multiple victims with gunshot wounds from various caliber weapons, wide-spread casualties from gunshot wounds and care delay, and non-firearm-related injuries associated with attempts to escape (lacerations, fractures).

Protective Equipment and Barriers

First responders should consider wearing protective equipment to mitigate ballistic, respiratory and mucous membrane, and dermal hazards. Utilizing available barriers or structural walls can also provide protective cover and/or concealment for first responders within the shooter's field of fire. Ballistic protective equipment includes soft body armor and ceramic plate body armor, and may also provide some level of protection should the active shooter event be combined with a secondary or subsequent IED attack. Experience indicates attackers may plan to detonate secondary or subsequent IEDs that target first responders or receiving hospitals.

Considerations for first responder ballistic protective equipment should include what type of equipment is best suited for EMS responders and when it should be worn (every shift, during times of high risk [e.g., on duty at a sports stadium], or just in response to IED events).

Protective Equipment Commonly Worn

Most law enforcement officers responding to the incident will be wearing Type II or IIIA bullet resistant vests, designed to stop bullets from most handguns, and shotgun pellets. First responders other than law enforcement typically do not wear ballistic protective equipment. Civilians at public places such will not be wearing any form of ballistic protective equipment.

Protective Equipment Risk Mitigation Considerations

Responders should utilize the highest level of protective equipment available to them — ideally Type IV ballistic vests and helmets. The NIJ body armor standard specifies ballistic threats that body armor must reliably protect against.[66][67]

Response and Incident Management Considerations

Maximize interoperability to the extent possible (through prior MOUs/MOAs/SOPs) to reduce time from injury to treatment. Strive to communicate on common frequencies and use standardized terminology. Ensure all responders (regardless of discipline — EMS, fire, law enforcement) are trained and equipped to provide early, aggressive hemorrhage control; use body armor; and use more integrated response and incident management. Flexibility is key in how effectively aid is delivered to the injured — a single solution may not work best in all scenarios (i.e., law enforcement brings the injured out to safety, law enforcement escorts EMS/fire into transitional zones, law enforcement provides care).

Medical Response System

System-wide efforts should include activities ranging from self-care, buddy-care, and bystander care to regional and multi-state trauma responses. The efforts include prehospital emergency medical services, ground ambulances, rotary and fixed wing aircraft patient transport, designated trauma centers, hospitals, and rehabilitation facilities. Unlike the management of routine emergencies, the response to active shooter incidents will be extraordinary for the Nation's trauma and EMS systems.

Prehospital Emergency Medical Services Considerations

Patient-Based Considerations: The last decade of war has seen significant advances in the ability of prehospital care to impact the mortality of combat wounds. The ability to stop life-threatening bleeding from extremity wounds has been demonstrated to reduce the number of treatable exsanguination deaths. Civilian adoption of some military clinical practices that are a significant departure from traditional prehospital care is appropriate:

- Aggressive hemorrhage control — including use of tourniquets and, where appropriate, hemostatic agents
- Aggressive airway management, including "sit up and lean forward" airway positioning
- Training all first responders in self-care, buddy care, and bystander care

System-Wide Implications

Experience from terrorist attacks (active shooter incidents) occurring in other countries demonstrates common prehospital care system challenges, including multiple simultaneous attacks that cause an enormous number of casualties that exceed the available resources of EMS responders. The adoption of techniques that are suitable for use in self-care, buddy-care, bystander care, and care delivered by first responders is essential to extend the depth of responders available to provide immediate life-saving care.

EMS must rapidly and accurately triage casualties at the incident site and expeditiously transport those identified for "immediate care" into an appropriate hospital setting. It is imperative that pre-hospital triaging of wounded patients be as efficient and accurate as possible. Over-triage of patients over-taxes specialty centers that are designed to care for more significantly injured patients, while under-triaging of patients puts critically wounded patients into facilities that may not be able to provide the life-saving care needed. In addition to proper triage, care must be taken to regulate the transportation of casualties in order to direct victims to the hospital best suited for providing the necessary level of care for the type and severity of injuries they have sustained. Often the closest hospital is quickly overwhelmed by injured transported by ambulances, police cars, and privately owned vehicles, as well as the "walking wounded". Because the influx of patients to the nearest hospital is dictated by human behavior outside control of the system, the EMS system must recognize this likelihood and plan for redistribution of injured patients such that the closest hospital can return to maximum functionality as soon as possible. Incident managers should also anticipate the need to provide for safety and security with the arrival of injured persons' family members, the "psychologically shocked," and the media.

From a law enforcement perspective, the following should be considered:

- Law enforcement units should be trained in active shooter response, to include deployment of a contact team and a follow-on rescue team, depending on local resources and system configuration.
- All first responders (EMS, fire, and law enforcement) should be trained and practiced to work together in active shooter scenarios.
- Active shooter first response should focus on traditional Care Under Fire injuries with immediate "Extraction" from the site of the attack as a priority. All casualties should be directed or moved to a "Safe Point" (a secure location near the attack) by extraction teams where the casualties will be retriaged and treated for transfer.
- Interoperability between EMS, fire, and law enforcement personnel must be exercised, and an understanding of the responsibilities and actions of all parties is essential. This is achieved through mutual trainings, well-developed policies, and tabletop exercises.
- State and local officials should promote CERTs to deliver civilian training in conjunction with non-governmental organizations.

Hospital-Based Trauma System Considerations

Hospital challenges experienced in foreign and domestic active shooter incidents include:

- Difficulty in acquiring information from the scene

- Maldistribution of patients (e.g., two of 15 hospitals receiving approximately 60 percent of casualties from the scene in one large-scale event)
- A requirement for large numbers of hospital medical personnel to adequately treat the wounded
- The need to implement mass casualty contingency plans at every point of care (e.g., radiology postponing imaging an ankle sprain to rule out a fracture)
- Concern that the hospital may be a target
- Activation of Mass Transfusion Protocols, based on scope of injuries
- Activation of staff augmentation/call back plans, based on scope of injuries
- Initiation of patient movement/transfer plans, based on scope of injuries

Medical leaders of responses to attacks have noted that in many cases the majority of the injured and dead from large events present at the hospital closest to the scene. Patients able to leave the scene may forego EMS triage and present at hospitals before more severely injured patients arrive. The large influx of patients may exceed the hospital's capability to provide care, resulting in a "functional collapse" from inability to meet the demand spike. When this occurs, there is a compelling need to redistribute patients.

Distribution of patients among hospitals, so that no one hospital exceeds its resources, is a key principle in addressing medical surge capacity following bombing attacks that result in a significant number of casualties.

To address the large number of patients arriving at local facilities, local hospitals will need the swift assistance of incoming health care providers to assist with re-triage of the arriving casualties and the provision of appropriate services to patients. This influx will include additional doctors, nurses, medical specialists, such as blood bank technologists and respiratory therapists, mental health providers, and chaplains. In addition, there will likely be the need for law enforcement personnel to maintain order and security. In the hours immediately after the blast, these additional personnel will likely come from surrounding communities and may include health care professionals from beyond the local area. While pre-event planning for cross-town (local) hospital credentialing and privileging of responding health care professionals can be arranged with relative ease, the issue of expeditious out-of-state credentialing and privileging of medical professionals responding to natural or manmade disasters can be more challenging.

Patient Movement/Transfer Considerations

As the patient load builds at local hospitals, some of the critically injured patients should be moved to other medical care facilities to optimize patient care. This will include movement to Level-1 trauma centers and other hospitals to better balance inpatient bed, operating room, intensive care unit, and rehabilitation bed utilization. Depending on the locality of the incident, this may include moving patients to other communities or across state lines. Long-distance transport of acutely injured patients will likely require aeromedical evacuation capabilities.

Provide First Aid After Improvised Explosive Device and/or Active Shooter Incidents:

STOP THE BLEEDING AND PROTECT THE WOUND

General

The longer a service member bleeds from a major wound, the less likely he will be able to survive his injuries. It is, therefore, important that the first aid provider promptly stop the external bleeding.

Clothing

In evaluating the casualty for location, type, and size of the wound or injury, cut or tear his clothing and carefully expose the entire area of the wound. This procedure is necessary to properly visualize injury and avoid further contamination. Clothing stuck to the wound should be left in place to avoid further injury. DO NOT touch the wound; keep it as clean as possible.

WARNING

DO NOT REMOVE protective clothing in a chemical environment. Apply dressings over the protective clothing.

Entrance and Exit Wounds

Before applying the dressing, carefully examine the casualty to determine if there is more than one wound. A missile may have entered at one point and exited at another point. The *EXIT* wound is usually *LARGER* than the entrance wound.

WARNING

The casualty should be continually monitored for development of conditions which may require the performance of necessary basic lifesaving measures, such as clearing the airway and mouth-to-mouth resuscitation. All open (or penetrating) wounds should be checked for a point of entry and exit and first aid measures applied accordingly.

WARNING

If the missile lodges in the body (fails to exit), DO NOT attempt to remove it or probe the wound. Apply a dressing. If there is an object extending from (impaled in) the wound, DO NOT remove the object. Apply a dressing around the object and use additional improvised bulky materials/dressings (use the cleanest material available) to build up the area around the object to stabilize the object and prevent further injury. Apply a supporting bandage over the bulky materials to hold them in place.

Field Dressing

- *a.* Use the casualty's field dressing; remove it from the wrapper and grasp the tails of the dressing with both hands (Figure 2-20).

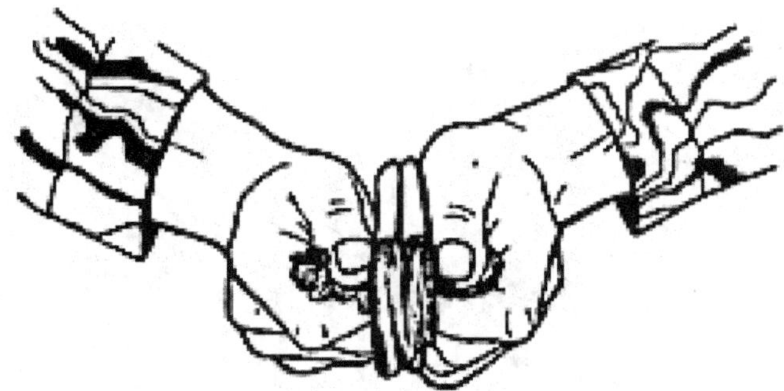

Figure 2-20. Grasping tails of dressing with both hands.

WARNING

DO NOT touch the white (sterile) side of the dressing, and DO NOT allow it to come in contact with any surface other than the wound.

- *b.* Hold the dressing directly over the wound with the white side down. Pull the dressing open (Figure 2-21) and place it directly over the wound (Figure 2-22).

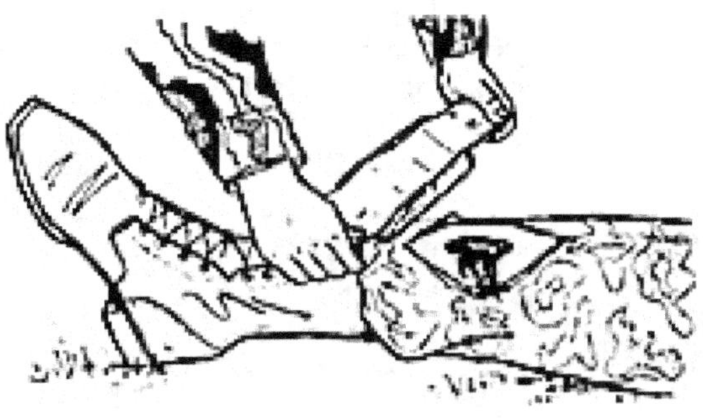

Figure 2-21. Pulling dressing open.

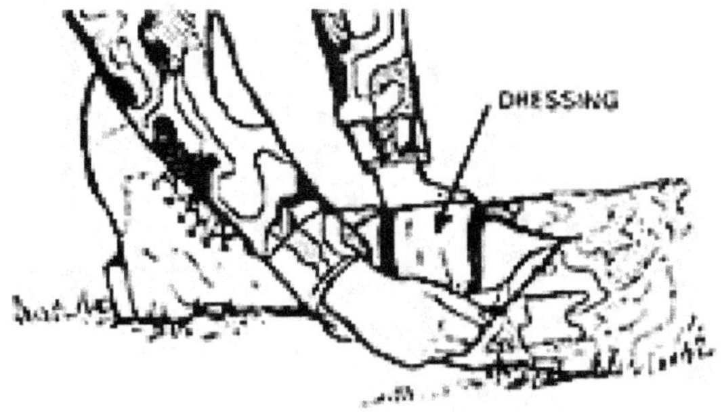

- *c.* Hold the dressing in place with one hand. Use the other hand to wrap one of the tails around the injured part, covering about one-half of the dressing (Figure 2-23). Leave enough of the tail for a knot. If the casualty is able, he may assist by holding the dressing in place.

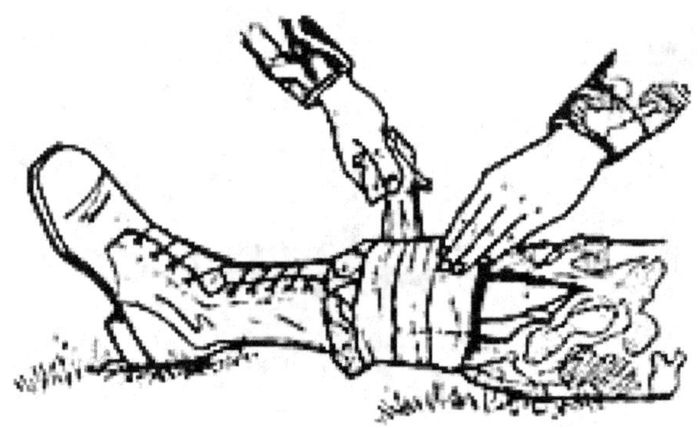

Figure 2-23. Wrapping tail of dressing around injured part.

- *d.* Wrap the other tail in the opposite direction until the remainder of the dressing is covered. The tails should seal the sides of the dressing to keep foreign material from getting under it.
- *e.* Tie the tails into a nonslip knot over the outer edge of the dressing (Figure 2-24). **DO NOT TIE THE KNOT OVER THE WOUND.** In order to allow blood to flow to the rest of an injured limb, tie the dressing firmly enough to prevent it from slipping but without causing a tourniquetlike effect; that is, the skin beyond the injury should not becomes cool, blue, or numb.

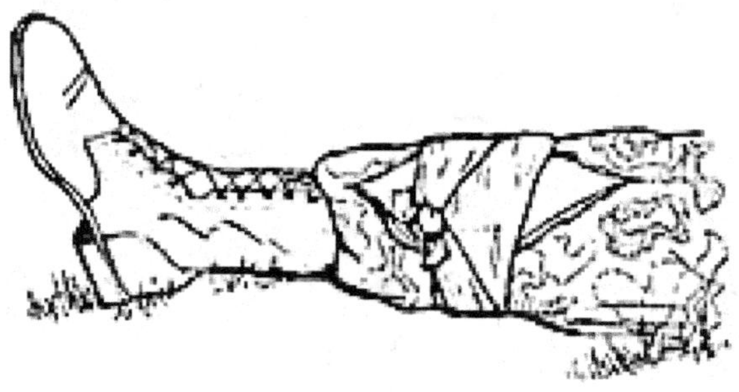

Figure 2-24. Tails tied into nonslip knot.

Manual Pressure

- *a.* If bleeding continues after applying the sterile field dressing, direct manual pressure may be used to help control bleeding. Apply such pressure by placing a hand on the dressing and exerting firm pressure for 5 to 10 minutes (Figure 2-25). The casualty may be asked to do this himself if he is conscious and can follow instructions.

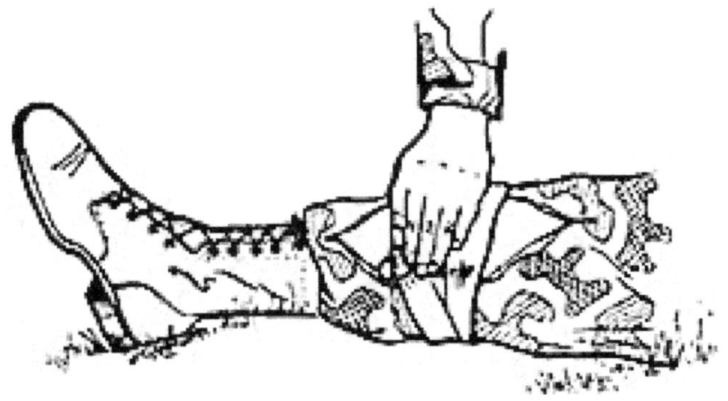

Figure 2-25. Direct manual pressure applied.

- *b.* Elevate an injured limb slightly above the level of the heart to reduce the bleeding (Figure 2-26).

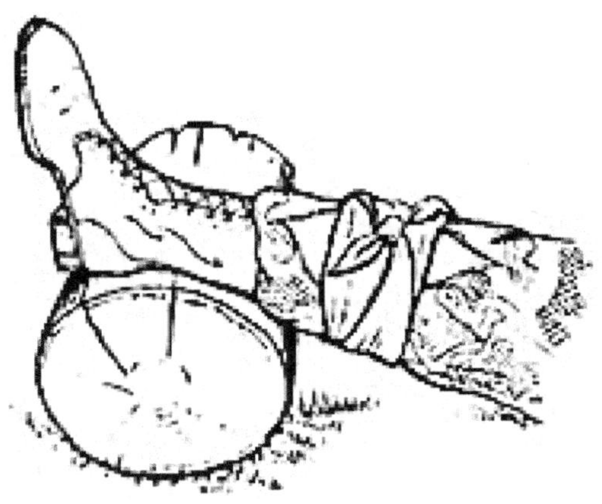

Figure 2-26. Injured limb elevated.

WARNING

DO NOT elevate a suspected fractured limb unless it has been properly splinted.

- *c.* If the bleeding stops, check shock; administer first aid for shock as necessary. If the bleeding continues, apply a pressure dressing.

Pressure Dressing

Pressure dressings aid in blood clotting and compress the open blood vessel. If bleeding continues after the application of a field dressing, manual pressure, and elevation, then a pressure dressing must be applied as follows:

- *a.* Place a wad of padding on top of the field dressing, directly over the wound (Figure 2-27). Keep the injured extremity elevated.

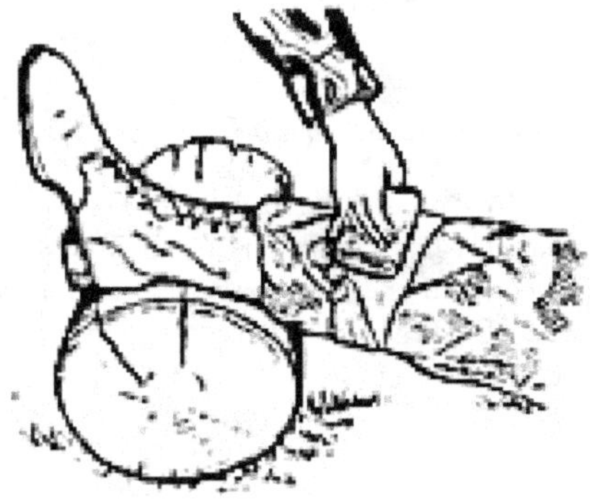

Figure 2-27. Wad of padding on top of field dressing.

NOTE

> Improvised bandages may be made from strips of cloth. These strips may be made from T-shirts, socks, or other garments.

- *b.* Place an improvised dressing (or cravat, if available) over the wad of padding (Figure 2-28). Wrap the ends tightly around the injured limb, covering the previously placed field dressing (Figure 2-29).

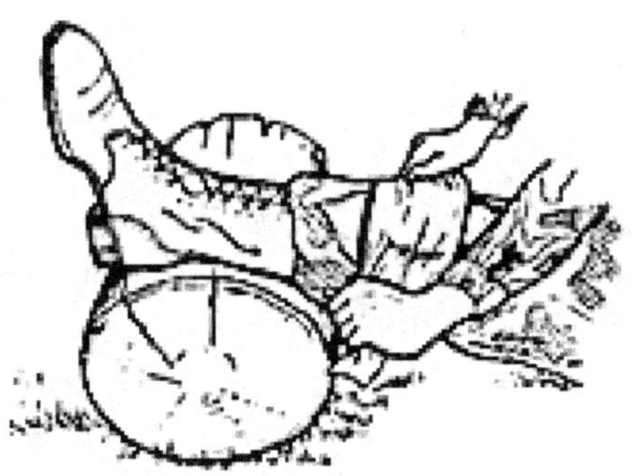

Figure 2-28. Improvised dressing over wad of padding

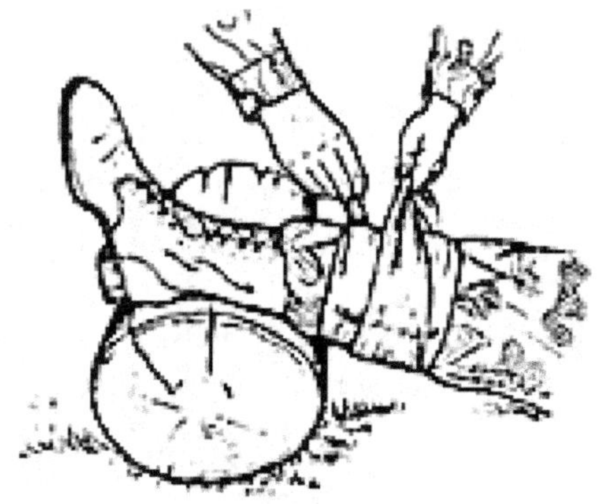

Figure 2-29. Ends of improvised dressing wrapped tightly around limb.

- *c.* Tie the ends together in a nonslip knot, directly over the wound site (Figure 2-30). DO NOT tie so tightly that it has a tourniquet-like effect. If bleeding continues and all other measures have failed, or if the limb is severed, then apply a tourniquet. Use the tourniquet as a **LAST RESORT**. When the bleeding stops, check for shock; administer first aid for shock as necessary.

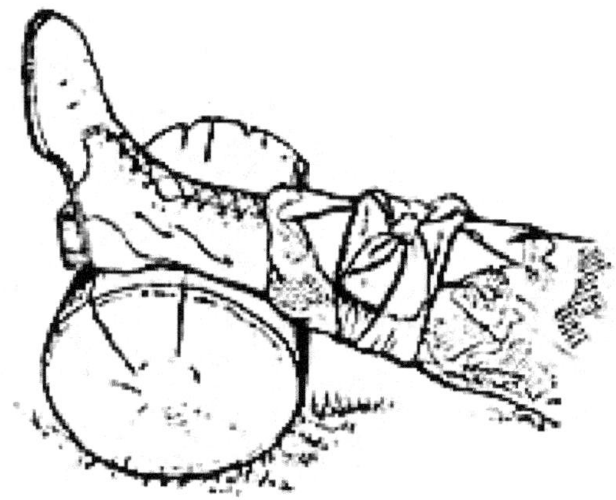

Figure 2-30. Ends of improvised dressing tied together in nonslip knot.

NOTE

Distal end of wounded extremities (fingers and toes) should be checked periodically for adequate circulation. The dressing must be loosened if the extremity becomes cool, blue, or numb.

NOTE

If bleeding continues and all other measures have failed (dressings and covering wound, applying direct manual pressure, elevating the limb above the heart level, and applying a pressure dressing while maintaining limb elevation) *then apply digital pressure*

Digital Pressure

Digital pressure (often called "pressure points") is an alternative method to control bleeding. This method uses pressure from the fingers, thumbs, or hands to press at the site or point where a main artery supplying the wounded area lies near the skin surface or over bone (Figure 2-31). This pressure may help shut off or slow down the flow of blood from the heart to the wound and is used in combination with direct pressure and elevation. It may help in instances where bleeding is not easily controlled, where a pressure dressing has not yet been applied, or where pressure dressings are not readily available.

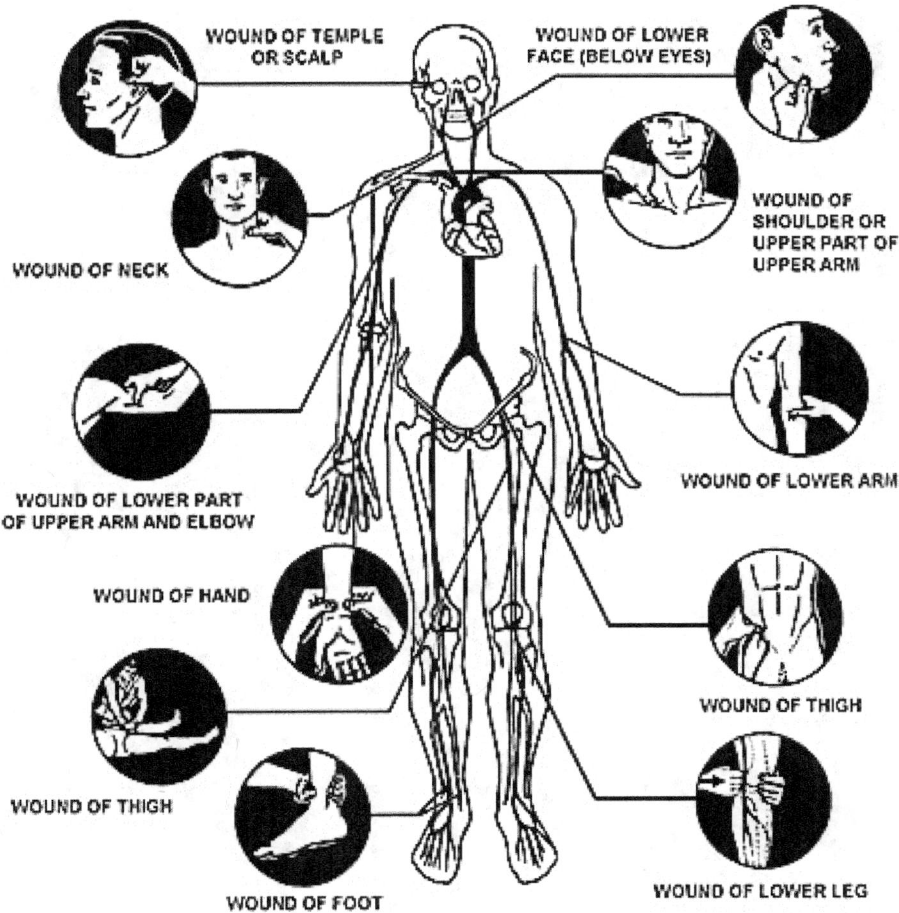

Figure 2-31. Digital pressure (pressure with fingers, thumbs or hands).

Tourniquet

DANGER

A tourniquet is only used on an arm or leg where there is a danger of the casualty losing his life (bleeding to death).

A tourniquet is a constricting band placed around an arm or leg to control bleeding. A service member whose arm or leg has been completely amputated may not be bleeding when first discovered, but a tourniquet should be applied anyway. This absence of bleeding is due to the body's normal defenses (contraction or clotting of blood vessels) as a result of the amputation, but after a period of time bleeding will start as the blood vessels relax or the clot may be knocked loose by moving the casualty. Bleeding from a major artery of the thigh, lower leg, or arm and bleeding from multiple arteries (which occurs in a traumatic amputation) may prove to be beyond control by manual pressure. If the pressure dressing under firm hand pressure becomes soaked with blood and the wound continues to bleed, apply a tourniquet.

WARNING

Casualty should be continually monitored for development of conditions which may require the performance of necessary basic lifesaving measures, such as: clearing the airway, performing mouth-tomouth resuscitation, preventing shock, and/or bleeding control. All open (or penetrating) wounds should be checked for a point of entry or exit and treated accordingly.

The tourniquet should not be used unless a pressure dressing has failed to stop the bleeding or an arm or leg has been cut off. On occasion, tourniquets have injured blood vessels and nerves. If left in place too long, a tourniquet can cause loss of an arm or leg. Once applied, it must stay in place, and the casualty must be taken to the nearest MTF as soon as possible. *DO NOT loosen or release a tourniquet after it has been applied as release could precipitate bleeding and potentially lead to shock.*

- *a. Improvising a Tourniquet.* In the absence of a specially designed tourniquet, a tourniquet may be made from a strong, pliable material, such as gauze or muslin bandages, clothing, or cravats. An improvised tourniquet is used with a rigid stick-like object. To minimize skin damage, ensure that the improvised tourniquet is at least 2 inches wide.

WARNING

The tourniquet must be easily identified or easily seen.

WARNING

DO NOT use wire or shoestring for a tourniquet band.

- *b. Placing the Improvised Tourniquet.*

- – (1) Place the tourniquet around the limb, between the wound and the body trunk (or between the wound and the heart). Never place it directly over a wound, a fracture, or joint. Tourniquets, for maximum effectiveness, should be placed on the upper arm or above the knee on the thigh (Figure 2-32).

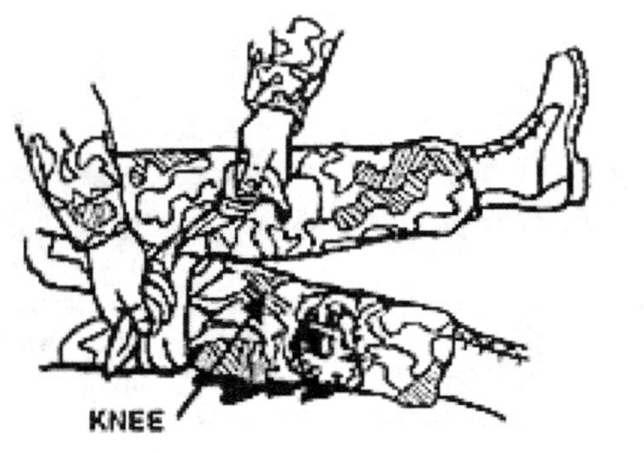

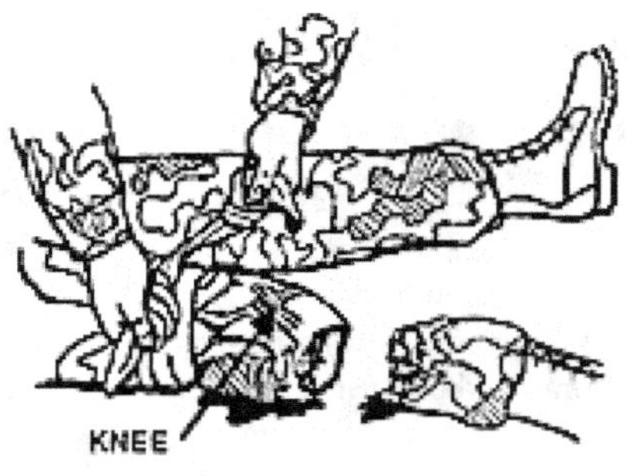

Figure 2-32. Tourniquet above knee.

- (2) The tourniquet should be well-padded. If possible, place the tourniquet over the smoothed sleeve or trouser leg to prevent the skin from being pinched or twisted. If the tourniquet is long enough, wrap it around the limb several times, keeping the material as flat as possible. Damaging the skin may deprive the surgeon of skin required to cover an amputation. Protection of the skin also reduces pain.

- *c. Applying the Tourniquet.*

- (1) Tie a half-knot. (A half-knot is the same as the first part of tying a shoe lace.)
- (2) Place a stick (or similar rigid object) on top of the halfknot (Figure 2-33).

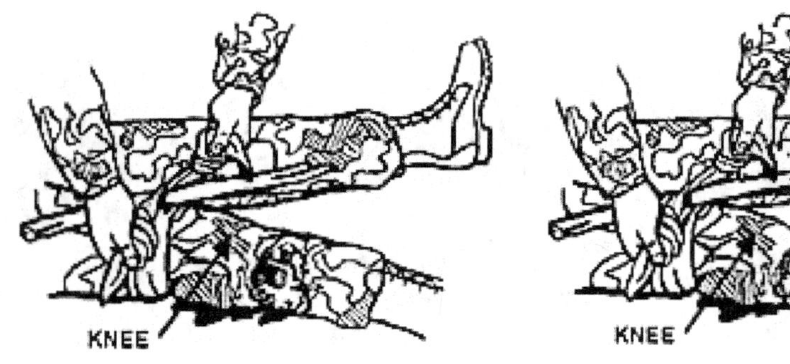

Figure 2-33. Rigid object on top of half-knot.

- (3) Tie a full knot over the stick (Figure 2-34).

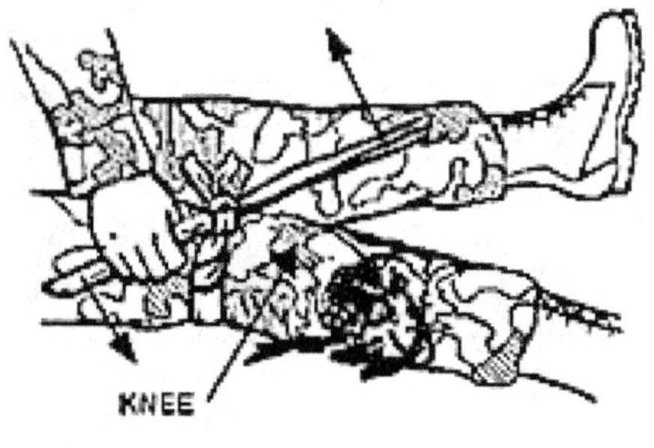

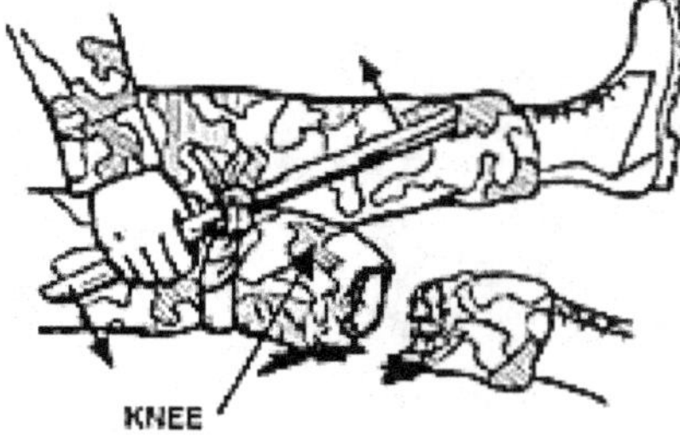

Figure 2-34. Full knot over rigid object.

– (4) Twist the stick (Figure 2-35) until the tourniquet is tight around the limb and/or the bright red bleeding has stopped. In the case of amputation, dark oozing blood may continue for a short time. This is the blood trapped in the area between the wound and tourniquet.

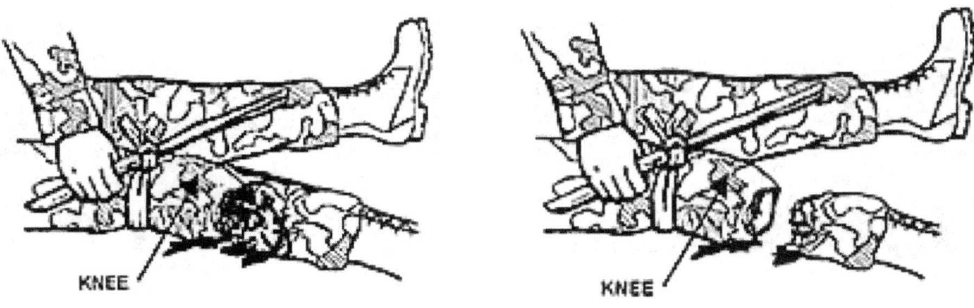

Figure 2-35. Stick twisted.

– (5) Fasten the tourniquet to the limb by looping the free ends of the tourniquet over the ends of the stick. Then bring the ends around the limb to prevent the stick from loosening. Tie them together on the side of the limb (Figure 2-36).

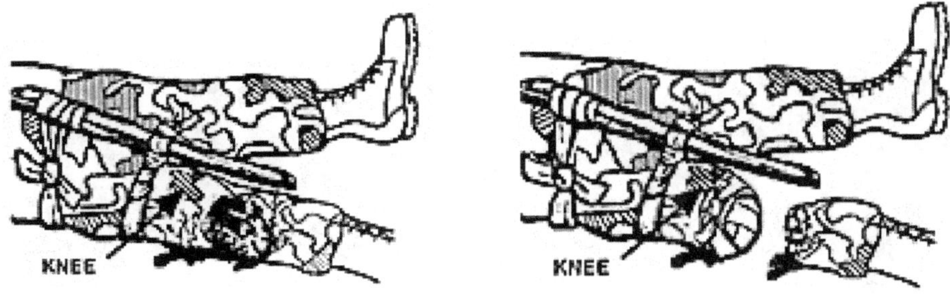

Figure 2-36. Tie free ends on side of limb.

NOTE

Other methods of securing the stick may be used as long as the stick does not unwind and no further injury results.

NOTE

If possible, save and transport any severed (amputated) limbs or body parts with (but out of sight of) the casualty.

- (6) DO NOT cover the tourniquet — you should leave it in full view. If the limb is missing (total amputation), apply a dressing to the stump. All wounds should have a dressing to protect the wound from contamination.

- (7) Mark the casualty's forehead with a "T" and the time to indicate a tourniquet has been applied. If necessary, use the casualty's blood to make this mark.

- (8) Check and treat for shock.

- (9) Seek medical aid.

CAUTION

Only appropriately skilled medical personnel may adjust or otherwise remove/release the tourniquet in the appropriate setting.

First Aid for Specific Injuries

General

Some wounds and burns will require special precautions and procedures when applying these measures. This chapter discusses specific first aid procedures for wounds of the head, face, and neck; chest and stomach wounds; and burns. It also discusses the techniques for applying dressings and bandages to specific parts of the body.

Head, Neck, and Facial Injuries

- *a. Head Injuries.*

  - (1) Head injuries range from minor abrasions or cuts on the scalp to severe brain injuries that may result in unconsciousness and sometimes death. Head injuries are classified as open or closed wounds. An open wound is one that is visible, has a break in the skin, and usually has evidence of bleeding. A closed wound may be visible (such as a depression in the skull) or the first aid provider may not be able to see any apparent injury (such as internal bleeding). Some head injuries result in unconsciousness; however, a service member may have a serious head wound and still be conscious. Casualties with head and neck injuries should be treated as though they also have a spinal injury. The casualty should not be moved until the head and neck is stabilized unless he is in immediate danger (such as close to a burning vehicle).

  - (2) Prompt first aid measures should be initiated for casualties with suspected head and neck injuries. The conscious casualty may be able to provide information on the extent of his injuries. However, as a result of the head injury, he may be confused and unable to provide accurate information. The signs and symptoms a first aid provider might observe are —

    - Nausea and vomiting.
    - Convulsions or twitches.
    - Slurred speech.
    - Confusion and loss of memory. (Does he know who he is? Does he know where he is? Does he know what day it is?)
    - Recent unconsciousness.
    - Dizziness.
    - Drowsiness.
    - Blurred vision, unequal pupils, or bruising (black eyes).
    - Paralysis (partial or full).
    - Complaint of headache.
    - Bleeding or other fluid discharge from the scalp, nose, or ears.
    - Deformity of the head (depression or swelling).
    - Staggering while walking.

- *b. Neck Injuries.* Neck injuries may result in heavy bleeding. Apply pressure above and below the injury, *but do not interfere with the breathing process*, and attempt to control the bleeding. Apply a dressing. Always evaluate the casualty for a possible neck fracture/spinal cord injury; if suspected, seek medical treatment immediately.

NOTE

Establish and maintain the airway in cases of facial or neck injuries. If a neck fracture or spinal cord injury is suspected, immobilize the injury and, if necessary, perform basic life support measures.

- *c. Facial Injuries.* Soft tissue injuries of the face and scalp are common. Abrasions (scrapes) of the skin cause no serious problems. Contusions (injury without a break in the skin) usually cause swelling. A contusion of the scalp looks and feels like a lump.

Laceration (cut) and avulsion (torn away tissue) injuries are also common. Avulsions are frequently caused when a sharp blow separates the scalp from the skull beneath it. Because the face and scalp are richly supplied with blood vessels (arteries and veins), wounds of these areas usually bleed heavily.

General First Aid Measures

- *a. General Considerations.* The casualty with a head injury (or suspected head injury) should be continually monitored for the development of conditions that *may require* basic lifesaving measures. After initiating first aid measures, request medical assistance and evacuation. If dedicated medical evacuation assets are not available, transport the casualty to an MTF as soon as the situation permits. The first aid provider should not attempt to remove a protruding object from the head or give the casualty anything to eat or drink. Further, the first aid provider should be prepared to —

    - • Clear the airway.
    - • Control bleeding (external).
    - • Administer first aid measures for shock.
    - • Keep the casualty warm.
    - • Protect the wound.

- *b . Unconscious Casualty.* An unconscious casualty does not have control of all of his body's functions and may choke on his tongue, blood, vomitus, or other substances. (Refer to Figure 2-39.)

    - (1) *Breathing.* The brain requires a constant supply of oxygen. A bluish (or in an individual with dark skin — grayish) color of skin around the lips and nail beds indicates that the casualty is not receiving enough oxygen. Immediate action must be taken to clear the airway, to position the casualty on his side, or to initiate rescue breathing.
    - (2) *Bleeding.* Bleeding from a head injury usually comes from blood vessels within the scalp. Bleeding can also develop inside the skull or within the brain. In most instances visible bleeding from the head can be controlled by application of the field first aid dressing.

• CAUTION

DO NOT *attempt to put unnecessary pressure on the wound or attempt to push any brain matter back into the head (skull).* **DO NOT** *apply a pressure dressing.*

- *c . Concussion.* If an individual receives a heavy blow to the head or face, he may suffer a brain concussion (an injury to the brain that involves a temporary loss of some or all of the brain's ability to function). For example, the casualty may not breathe properly for a short period of time, or he may become confused and stagger when he attempts to walk. Symptoms of a concussion may only last for a short period of time. However, if a casualty is suspected of having suffered a concussion, he should be transported to an MTF as soon as conditions permit.

- *d. Convulsions.* Convulsions (seizures/involuntary jerking) may occur even after a mild head injury. When a casualty is convulsing, protect him from hurting himself. Take the following measures:

    - (1) Ease him to the ground if he is standing or sitting.
    - (2) Support his head and neck.
    - (3) Maintain his airway.
    - (4) Protect him from further injury (such as hitting close-by objects).

> **DO NOT** forcefully hold the arms and legs if they are jerking because this can lead to broken bones. **DO NOT** force anything between the casualty's teeth — especially if they are tightly clenched because this may obstruct the casualty's airway. Maintain the casualty's airway if necessary.

- *e. Brain Damage.* In *severe* head injuries where brain tissue is protruding, *leave the wound alone*; carefully place a loose moistened dressing (moistened with sterile normal saline if available) and also a first aid dressing over the tissue to protect it from further contamination. **DO NOT** *remove or disturb any foreign matter that may be in the wound.* Position the casualty so that his head is higher than his body. Keep him warm and *seek medical assistance immediately.*

> If there is an object extending from the wound, **DO NOT** remove the object. Improvise bulky dressings from the cleanest material available and place this material around the protruding object for support, then apply the field dressing.

Chest Wounds

Blunt trauma, bullet or missile wounds, stab wounds, or falls may cause chest injuries. These injuries can be serious and may cause death quickly if first aid is not administered in a timely manner. A casualty with a chest injury may complain of pain in the chest or shoulder area; he may have difficulty breathing. His chest may not rise normally when he breathes. The injury may cause the casualty to cough up blood and to have a rapid or a weak heartbeat. A casualty with an open chest wound has a punctured chest wall. The sucking sound heard when he breathes is caused by air leaking into his chest cavity. This particular type of wound is dangerous and will collapse the injured lung (Figure 3-1). Breathing becomes difficult for the casualty because the wound is open. The service members life may depend upon how quickly you apply an occlusive dressing over the wound.

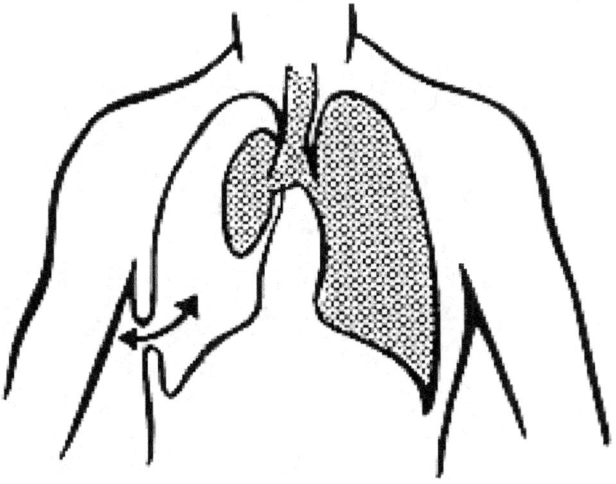

Figure 3-1. Collapsed lung.

First Aid for Chest Wounds

- *a . Evaluate the Casualty.* Be prepared to perform first aid measures. These measures may include clearing the airway, rescue breathing, treatment for shock, and/or bleeding control.
- *b . Expose the Wound.* If appropriate, cut or remove the casualty's clothing to expose the wound. Remember, **DO NOT** remove clothing that is stuck to the wound because additional injury may result. **DO NOT** attempt to clean the wound.

NOTE

Examine the casualty to see if there is an entry and exit wound. If there are two wounds (entry, exit), perform the same procedure for both wounds. Treat the more serious (heavier bleeding, larger) wound first. It may be necessary to improvise a dressing for the second wound by using strips of cloth, such as a torn T-shirt, or whatever material is available. Also, listen for sucking sounds to determine if the chest wall is punctured.

CAUTION

*If there is an object impaled in the wound, **DO NOT** remove it. Apply a dressing around the object and use additional improvised bulky materials/dressings (use the cleanest materials available) to build up the area around the object. Apply a supporting bandage over the bulky materials to hold them in place.*

CAUTION

DO NOT REMOVE *protective clothing in a chemical environment. Apply dressings over the protective clothing.*

- *c . Open the Casualty's Field Dressing Plastic Wrapper.* In cases where there is a sucking chest wound, the plastic wrapper is used with the field dressing to create an occlusive dressing. If a plastic wrapper is not available, or if an additional wound needs to be treated; cellophane, foil, the casualty's poncho, or similar material may be used. The covering should be wide enough to extend 2 inches or more beyond the edges of the wound in all directions.

  - (1) Tear open one end of the casualty's plastic wrapper covering the field dressing. Be careful not to destroy the wrapper and **DO NOT** touch the inside of the wrapper.
  - (2) Remove the inner packet (field dressing).
  - (3) Complete tearing open the empty plastic wrapper using as much of the wrapper as possible to create a flat surface.

- *d. Place the Wrapper Over the Wound.* Place the inside surface of the plastic wrapper directly over the wound *when the casualty exhales* and hold it in place (Figure 3-2). The casualty may hold the plastic wrapper in place if he is able.

Figure 3-2. Open chest wound sealed with an occlusive dressing.

e. Apply the Dressing to the Wound.

    – (1) Use your free hand and shake open the field dressing (Figure 3-3).

Figure 3-3. Shaking open the field dressing.

– (2) Place the white side of the dressing on the plastic wrapper covering the wound (Figure 3-4).

NOTE

Use the casualty's field dressing, not your own.

– (3) Have the casualty breathe normally.

– (4) While maintaining pressure on the dressing, grasp one tail of the field dressing with the other hand and wrap it around the casualty's back. If tape is available, tape three sides of the plastic wrapper to the chest wall to provide occlusive type dressing. Leave one side untapped to provide emergency escape for air that may build up in the chest. If tape is not available, secure wrapper on three sides with field dressing leaving the fourth side as a flap.

– (5) Wrap the other tail in the opposite direction, bringing both tails over the dressing (Figure 3-5).

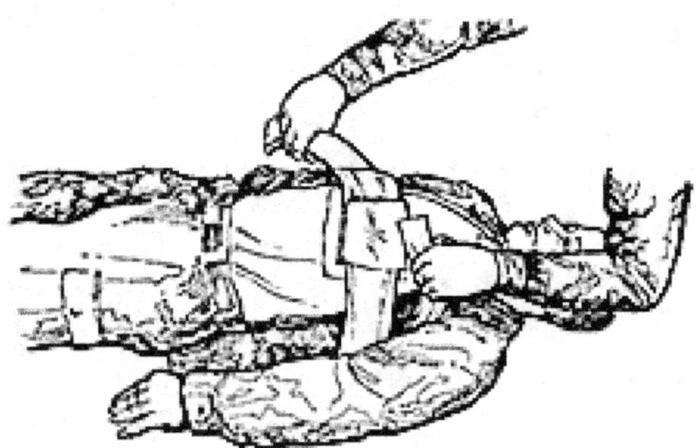

Figure 3-5. Tails of field dressing wrapped around casualty in opposite direction.

– (6) Tie the tails into a square knot in the center of the dressing *after* the casualty exhales and *before* he inhales. This will aid in maintaining pressure on the bandage after it has been tied (Figure 3-6). Tie the dressing firmly enough to secure the dressing without interfering with the casualty's breathing.

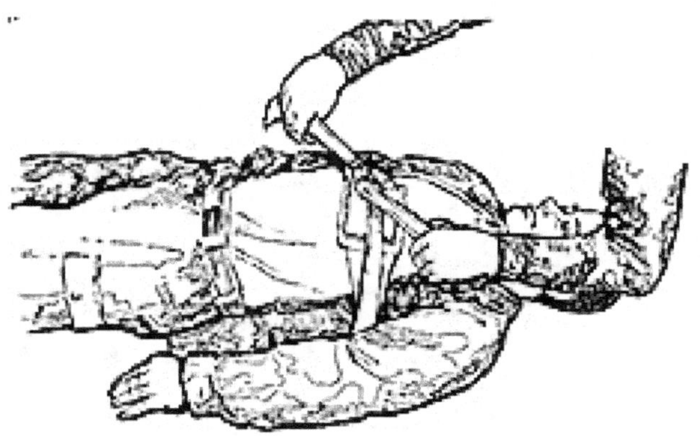

Figure 3-6. Tails of dressing tied into square knot over center of dressing.

NOTE

> When practical, apply direct manual pressure over the dressing for 5
> to 10 minutes to help control the bleeding.

- *f. Position the Casualty.* Position the casualty on his injured side or in a sitting position, whichever makes breathing easier (Figure 3-7).

-

Figure 3-7. Casualty positioned (lying) on injured side.

- *g. Seek Medical Assistance.* Contact medical personnel.

WARNING

If an occlusive dressing has been improperly placed, air may enter the chest cavity with no means of escape. This causes a life-threatening condition called tension pneumothorax. *If the casualty's condition (for example, difficulty breathing, shortness of breath, restlessness, or blueness/grayness of the skin) worsens after placing the dressing, quickly lift or remove, and then replace the occlusive dressing.*

Abdominal Wounds

The most serious abdominal wound is one in which an object penetrates the abdominal wall and pierces internal organs or large blood vessels. In these instances, bleeding may be severe and death can occur rapidly.

First Aid for Abdominal Wounds

- *a . Evaluate the Casualty.* Be prepared to perform basic first aid measures. Always check for both entry and exit wounds. If there are two wounds (entry and exit), treat the wound that appears more serious first (for example, the heavier bleeding, protruding organs, larger wound, and so forth). It may be necessary to improvise dressings for the second wound by using strips of cloth, a T-shirt, or the cleanest material available.
- *b . Position the Casualty.* Place and maintain the casualty on his back with his knees in an upright (flexed) position (Figure 3-8). The kneesup position helps relieve pain, assists in the treatment of shock, prevents further exposure of the bowel (intestines) or abdominal organs, and helps relieve abdominal pressure by allowing the abdominal muscles to relax.

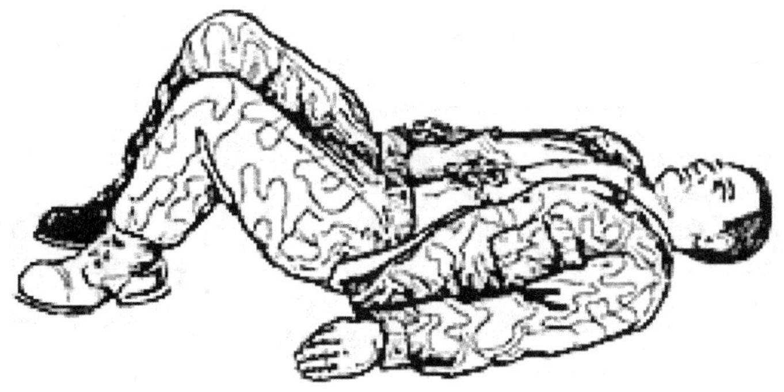

Figure 3-8. Casualty positioned (lying) on back with knees (flexed) up.

- *c. Expose the Wound.*

- – (1) Remove the casualty's loose clothing to expose the wound. However, **DO NOT** attempt to remove clothing that is stuck to the wound; removing it may cause further injury.

– CAUTION

DO NOT REMOVE *protective clothing in a chemical environment. Apply dressings* over *the protective clothing.*

- – (2) Gently pick up any organs that may be on the ground. Do this with a clean, dry dressing or with the cleanest available material. Place the organs on top of the casualty's abdomen (Figure 3-9).

Figure 3-9. Protruding organs placed near wound.

NOTE

> **DO NOT** probe, clean, or try to remove any foreign object from the abdomen.
> **DO NOT** touch with bare hands any exposed organs. **DO NOT** push organs back
> inside the body.

- *d . Apply the Field Dressing.* Use the casualty's field dressing, not your own. If the field dressing is not large enough to cover the entire wound, the plastic wrapper from the dressing may be used to cover the wound first (placing the field dressing on top). Open the plastic wrapper carefully without touching the inner surface. If necessary, other improvised dressings may be made from clothing, blankets, or the cleanest materials available.

WARNING

If there is an object extending from the wound, DO NOT remove it. Place as much of the wrapper over the wound as possible without dislodging or moving the object. DO NOT place the wrapper over the object.

- (1) Grasp the tails in both hands.
- (2) Hold the dressing with the white side down directly over the wound. **DO NOT** touch the white (sterile) side of the dressing or allow anything except the wound to come in contact with it.
- (3) Pull the dressing open and place it directly over the wound (Figure 3-10). If the casualty is able, he may hold the dressing in place.

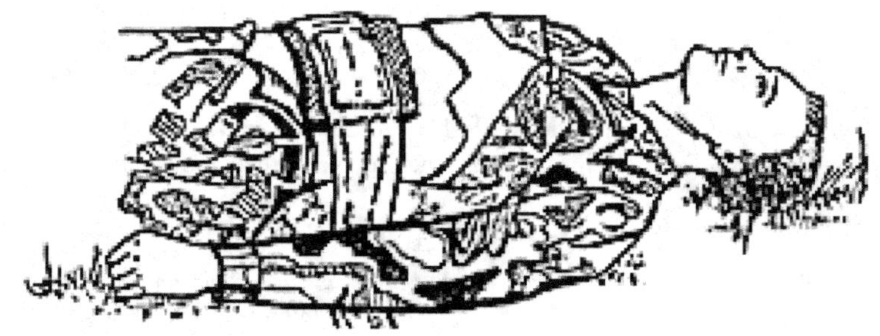

Figure 3-10. Dressing placed directly over the wound.

- (4) Hold the dressing in place with one hand and use the other hand to wrap one of the tails around the body.
- (5) Wrap the other tail in the opposite direction until the dressing is completely covered. Leave enough of the tail for a knot.
- (6) Loosely tie the tails with a square knot at the casualty's side (Figure 3-11).

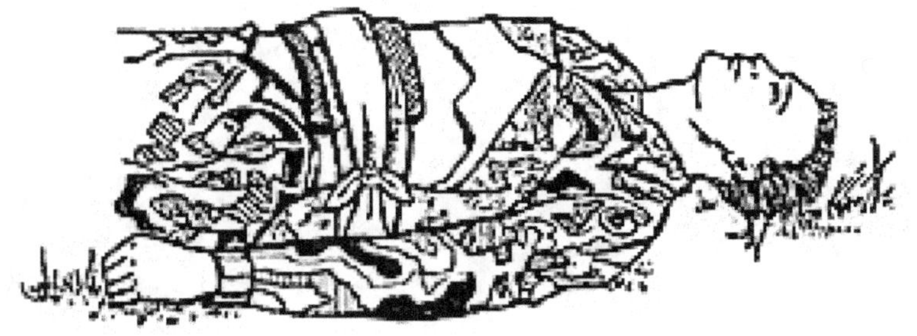

Figure 3-11. Dressing applied and tails tied with a square knot.

WARNING

When the dressing is applied, DO NOT put pressure on the wound or exposed internal parts, because pressure could cause further injury (vomiting, ruptured intestines, and so forth). Therefore, tie the dressing ties (tails) loosely at casualty's side, not directly over the dressing.

- (7) Tie the dressing firmly enough to prevent slipping without applying pressure to the wound site (Figure 3-12).

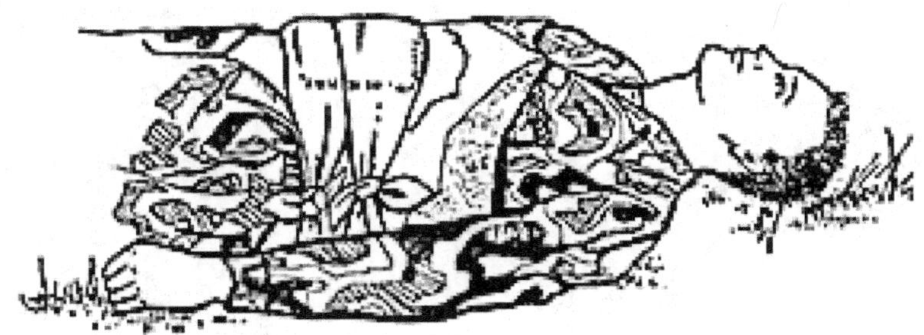

Figure 3-12. Field dressing covered with improvised material and loosely tied.

Field dressings can be covered with improvised reinforcement material (cravats, strips of torn T-shirt, or other cloth) for additional support and protection. Tie improvised bandage on the opposite side of the dressing ties firmly enough to prevent slipping but without applying additional pressure to the wound.

CAUTION

DO NOT *give casualties with abdominal wounds food or water (moistening the lips is allowed).*

- *e. Seek Medical Assistance.* Notify medical personnel.

Burn Injuries

Burns often cause extreme pain, scarring, or even death. Before administering first aid, you must be able to recognize the type of burn. There are four types of burns:

- • Thermal burns caused by fire, hot objects, hot liquids, and gases; or by nuclear blast or fireball.
- • Electrical burns caused by electrical wires, current, or lightning.
- • Chemical burns caused by contact with wet or dry chemicals or white phosphorus (WP) — from marking rounds and grenades.
- • Laser burns (eye [ocular] injury).

First Aid for Burns

- *a . Eliminate the Source of the Burn.* The source of the burn must be eliminated before any evaluation of the casualty can occur and first aid administered.

  - (1) Quickly remove the casualty from danger and cover the *thermal burn* with any large nonsynthetic material, such as a field jacket. If the casualty's clothing is still on fire, roll the casualty on the ground to smother (put out) the flames (Figure 3-13).

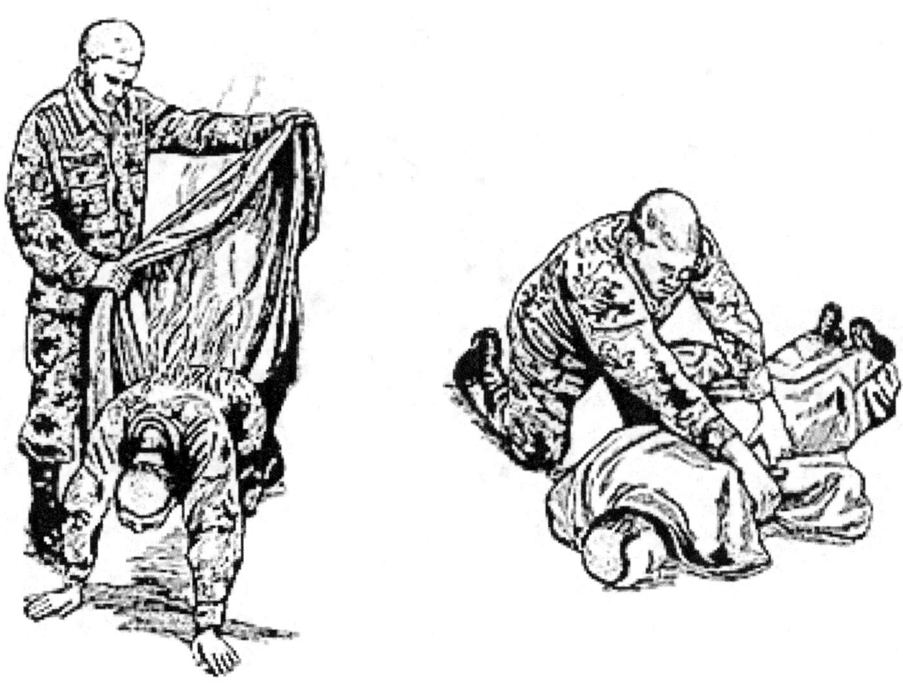

Figure 3-13. Casualty covered and rolled on ground.
CAUTION
Synthetic materials, such as nylon, may melt and cause further injury.

- (2) Remove the *electrical burn* casualty from the electrical source by turning off the electrical current. **DO NOT** attempt to turn off the electricity if the source is not close by. Speed is critical, so **DO NOT** waste unnecessary time. If the electricity cannot be turned off, wrap any *nonconductive* material (*dry* rope, clothing, wood, and so forth) around the casualty's back and shoulders and drag the casualty away from the electrical source (Figure 3-14). **DO NOT** make body-to-body contact with the casualty or touch any wires because you could also become an electrical burn casualty.

Figure 3-14. Casualty removed from electrical source (using nonconductive material).

WARNING

High voltage electrical burns may cause temporary unconsciousness, difficulties in breathing, or difficulties with the heart (heartbeat).

- (3) Remove the *chemical* from the *burned casualty*. Remove *liquid* chemicals by flushing with as much water as possible. Remove *dry* chemicals by brushing off loose particles (**DO NOT** use the bare surface of your hand because you could become a chemical burn casualty) and then flush with large amounts of water, if available. If large amounts of water are not available, then **NO** water should be applied because small amounts of water applied to a dry chemical burn may cause a chemical reaction. When WP strikes the skin, smother with a wet cloth or mud. Keep WP covered with a wet material to exclude air; this should help prevent the particles from burning.

- (4) Remove the *laser burn* casualty from the source. When removing the casualty from the laser beam source, be careful not to enter the beam or you may become a casualty. Never look directly at the beam source and if possible, wear appropriate eye protection.

NOTE

After the casualty is removed from the source of the burn, he should be evaluated for conditions requiring basic first aid measures.

- *b* . *Expose the Burn*. Cut and gently lift away any clothing covering the burned area, without pulling clothing over the burns. Leave in place any clothing that is stuck to the burn. If the casualty's hands or wrists have been burned, remove jewelry if possible without causing further injury (rings, watches, and so forth) and place in his pockets. This prevents the necessity to cut off jewelry since swelling usually occurs as a result of a burn.

CAUTION

DO NOT *lift or cut away clothing if in a chemical environment. Apply the dressing directly over the casualty's protective clothing.* **DO NOT** *attempt to decontaminate skin where blisters have formed.*

- *c. Apply a Field Dressing to the Burn.*

  - (1) Grasp the tails of the casualty's dressing in both hands.
  - (2) Hold the dressing directly over the wound with the white side down, pull the dressing open, and place it directly over the wound. **DO NOT** touch the white (sterile) side of the dressing or allow anything except the wound to come in contact with it. If the casualty is able, he may hold the dressing in place.
  - (3) Hold the dressing in place with one hand and use the other hand to wrap one of the tails around the limbs or the body.
  - (4) Wrap the other tail in the opposite direction until the dressing is completely covered.
  - (5) Tie the tails into a square knot over the outer edge of the dressing. The dressing should be applied lightly over the burn. Ensure that dressing is applied firmly enough to prevent it from slipping.

NOTE

Use the cleanest improvised dressing material available if a field dressing is not available or if it is not large enough for the entire wound.

- *d* . *Take the Following Precautions*:

  - • **DO NOT** place the dressing over the face or genital area.
  - • **DO NOT** break the blisters.
  - • **DO NOT** apply grease or ointments to the burns.
  - • For electrical burns, check for both an entry and exit burn from the passage of electricity through the body. Exit burns may appear on any area of the body despite location of entry burn.
  - • For burns caused by wet or dry chemicals, flush the burns with large amounts of water and cover with a dry dressing.
  - • For burns caused by WP, flush the area with water, then cover with a wet material, dressing, or mud to exclude the air and keep the WP particles from burning.
  - • For laser burns, apply a field dressing.
  - • If the casualty is conscious and not nauseated, give him small amounts of water.

- *e. Seek Medical Assistance.* Notify medical personnel.

List of Major Bombing Incidents in the United States 2007-2017

- 26 October 2007, New York City, New York, 0 Dead, 0 Injured
- 6 March 2008, New York City, New York, 0 Dead, 0 Injured
- 4 May 2008, San Diego, CA, 0 Dead, 0 Injured
- 25 May 2009, New York City, New York, 0 Dead, 0 Injured
- 1 May 2010, New York City, New York, 0 Dead, 0 Injured
- 25 November 2010, Portland, Oregon, 0 Dead, 0 Injured
- 15 April 2013, Boston, Massachusetts, 6 Dead, 281 Injured
- 17-19 September 2016, New Yorkand New Jersey, 0 Dead, 35 Injured

List of Major Mass Shootings in the United States 2007-2017

- 12 February 2007, Trolley Square Mall, Salt Lake City, Utah, 6 Dead, 4 Injured
- 16 April 2007, Virginia Tech, Blacksburg, Virginia, 32 Dead, 23 Injured
- 5 December 2007, Westroads Mall, Omaha, Nebraska, 9 Dead, 6 Injured
- 9 December 2007, Youth With A Mission training center, Arvada, Colorado, 5 Dead, 5 Injured
- 7 February 2008, City Council, Kirkwood, Missouri, 7 Dead, 1 Injured
- 14 February 2008, Northern Illinois University, DeKalb, Illinois, 6 Dead, 21 Injured
- 25 June 2008, Atlantis Plastics factory, Henderson, Kentucky, 6 Dead, 1 Injured
- 27 July 2008, Tennessee Valley Unitarian Universalist Church, Knoxville, Tennessee, 2 Dead, 7 Injured
- 24 December 2008, Covina, Los Angeles, CA, 10 Dead, 3 Injured
- 10 March 2009, Geneva County, Alabama, 11 Dead, 6 Injured
- 29 March 2009, Pinelake Health and Rehabilitation nursing home, Carthage, North Carolina, 14 Dead, 4 Injured
- 3 April 2009, American Civic Association immigration center, Binghamton, New York, 14 Dead, 4 Injured
- 5 November 2009, Fort Hood, Texas, 13 Dead, 33 Injured
- 7 January 2010, ABB power plant, St. Louis, Missouri, 4 Dead, 5 Injured
- 8 January 2011, Casas Adobes, Arizona, 6 Dead, 15 Injured
- 7 July 2011, Grand Rapids, Michigan, 8 Dead, 2 Injured
- 3 August 2010, Manchester, Connecticut, 9 Dead, 2 Injured
- 7 August 2011, Copley Township, Ohio, 8 Dead, 1 Injured
- 6 September 2011, Carson City, Nevada, 5 Dead, 7 Injured
- 12 October 2011, Seal Beach, California, 8 Dead, 1 Injured
- 2 April 2012, Oikos University, Oakland, California, 7 Dead, 3 Injured
- 30 May 2012, Café Racer, Seattle, Washington, 6 Dead, 1 Injured
- 20 July 2012, Century 16 movie theater, Aurora, Colorado, 12 Dead, 70 Injured
- 5 August 2012, Sikh Temple, Oak Creek, Wisconsin, 7 Dead, 4 Injured
- 27 September 2012, Minneapolis, Minnesota, 7 Dead, 2 Injured
- 14 December 2012, Sandy Hook Elementary School, Newtown, Connecticut, 28 Dead, 2 Injured
- 7 June 2013, Santa Monica, California, 6 Dead, 4 Injured
- 26 July 2013, Todel Apartments, Hialeah, Florida, 7 Dead, 0 Injured
- 16 September 2013, Naval Sea Systems Command, Washington, D.C., 13 Dead, 8 Injured
- 2 April 2014, Fort Hood military base, Killeen, Texas, 4 Dead, 14 Injured
- 9 July 2014, Harris County, Texas, 6 Dead, 1 Injured
- 24 October 2014, Marysville Pilchuck High School, Marysville, Washington, 5 Dead, 3 Injured
- 26 February 2015, Tyrone, Missouri, 8 Dead, 1 Injured
- 17 May 2015, Twin Peaks restaurant, Waco, Texas, 9 Dead, 17 Injured
- 17 June 2015, Emanuel African Methodist Episcopal Church, Charleston, South Carolina, 9 Dead, 1 Injured
- 16 July 2015, Chattanooga, Tennessee, 6 Dead, 2 Injured
- 8 August 2015, Harris County, Texas, 8 Dead, 0 Injured
- 1 October 2015, Umpqua Community College, Roseburg, Oregon, 10 Dead, 9 Injured
- 2 December 2015, Inland Regional Center, San Bernardino, California, 16 Dead, 24 Injured
- 25 February 2016, Newton and Hesston, Kansas, 4 Dead, 14 Injured

- 9 March 2016, Wilkinsburg, Pennsylvania, 6 Dead, 3 Injured
- 21-22 April 2016, Pike County, Ohio, 8 Dead, 0 Injured
- 12 June 2016, Pulse, a gay nightclub, Orlando, Florida, 50 Dead, 53 Injured
- 7 July 2016, Dallas, Texas, 6 Dead, 11 Injured
- 6 January 2017, Fort Lauderdale – Hollywood International Airport, Broward County, Florida, 5 Dead, 42 Injured
- 26 March 2017, Cameo nightclub, Cincinnati, Ohio, 2 Dead, 16 Injured

Footnotes

1. Jacobs LM, McSwain NE Jr, et al. Improving survival from active shooter events: The Hartford Consensus. J Trauma Acute Care Surg. 2013 Jun;74(6):1399-1400. http://journals.lww.com/jtrauma/ Fulltext/2013/06000/Improving_survival_from_ active_shooter_events__.3.aspx.

2. START Global Terrorism Database [database online]. National Consortium for the Study of Terrorism and Responses to Terrorism. http://www.start.umd.edu/start/.

3. Committee for Tactical Emergency Casualty Care. http://c\protect\unhbox\voidb@x\penalty\@M\hskip\z@skip-\discretionary{}{}{}\penalty\@M\hskip\z@skip{}tecc.org/.

4. The Committee for Tactical Emergency Care (C-TECC): Evolution and Application of TCCC Guidelines to Civilian High Threat Medicine. JSOM, Vol 11, Ed 2;Spring/Summer 2011. https://www.jsomonline.org/PDFs/TECC.pdf Joint Committee to Create a National Policy to Enhance Survivability From Mass-Casualty Shooting Events.

5. Improving Survival from Active Shooter Events: The Hartford Consensus. *Bull Am Coll Surg.* 2013;98(6):14-16.

6. *TEMS Position Statement. http://ntoa.org/sections/tems/tems\protect\unhbox\voidb@x\penalty\@M\hskip\z@skip-\discretionary{}{}{}\penalty\@M\hskip\z@skip{}position\ protect\unhbox\voidb@x\penalty\@M\hskip\z@skip-\discretionary{}{}{}\penalty\@M\ hskip\z@skip{}statement/.*

7. Propper BW, Rasmussen TE, Davidson S, et al. Surgical response to multiple casualty incidents in the modern era. *Ann Surg* 2009;250(2):311-315.

8. http://www.usaisr.amedd.army.mil/cpgs.html.

9. Ho AM, Karmaker MK, Dion PW. Are we giving enough coagulation factors during major trauma resuscitation? *Am J Surg* 2005;190(3):479-84.

10. Borgman MA, Spinella PC, Perkins J, et al. The ratio of blood products transfused affects mortality in patients receiving massive transfusions at a combat support hospital. *J Trauma* 2007;63(4):805-13.

11. Gonzalez EA, Moore FA, Holcomb JB, et al. Fresh frozen plasma should be given earlier to patients requiring massive transfusion. *J Trauma* 2007;62(1):112-9.

12. Holcomb JB, Wade CE, Michalek JE, et al. Increased plasma and platelet to red blood cell ratios improves outcomes in 466 massively transfused civilian trauma patients. *Ann Surg* 2008;248:447-458.

13. DHS/DOJ, *Bomb Threat Stand-Off Card, Washington DC, 2014.*

14. Stein M. Urban bombing: A trauma surgeon's perspective. *Scand J Surg* 2005;94:286--292.

15. Kashuk JL, Halperin P, Caspi G, Colwell C, Moore EE. Evil creativity challenges our trauma systems. *J Am Coll Surg.* 2009 Jul;209(1):134-140.

16. Soffer D, Klausner J, Bar-Zohar D, et al. Usage of blood products in multiple-casualty incidents. The experence of a level I trauma center in Israel. *Arch Surg* 2008; 143(10):983-89.

17.	Einav S, Aharonson-Daniel L, Weissman C, et al. In-hospital resource utilization during multiple casualty incidents. *Ann Surg* 2006; 243(4):533-40.

18.	Aylwin T, Konig N, Brennan P, et al. Reduction in critical mortality in urban mass casualty incidents: analysis of triage, surge and resource use after the London bombings on July 7, 2005. *Lancet* 2006; (368) 9554:2219-25

19.	Peleg K, Aharonson-Daniel L, Michael M, et al. Patterns of injury in hospitalized terrorist victims. *Am J Emerg Med* 2003; 21(4):258-62.

20.	Turegano-Fuentes F, Caba-Doussoux P, Jover-Navalon J, et al. Injury patterns from major urban terrorist bombings in trains: the Madrid experience. *World J Surg* 2008;32(6):1168-75.

21.	*http://www.amtrauma.org/?page=BlastPrimer.*

22.	Morrissey J. EMS Response to Active Shooter Incidents. *EMS World*, July 2011: 42-48. http://emsworld.epubxp.com/i/35512/66.

23.	Nordberg M. When kids kill: Columbine High School shooting. *Emergency Medical Services.* Oct1999; 28(10):39-47, 49-50.

24.	Mass Shootings at Virginia Tech April 16, 2007, Report of the Virginia Tech Review Panel, August 2007. http://www.governor.virginia.gov/tempcontent/ techPanelReport\protect\unhbox\voidb@x\penalty\@M\hskip\z@skip-\ discretionary{}{}{}\penalty\@M\hskip\z@skip{}docs/FullReport.pdf.

25.	Report of the High Level Enquiry Committee (HLEC) on 26/11. Maharashtra Government vide GAD GR No: Raasua. 2008/C.R.34/29-A. http://timesofindia.indiatimes.com/photo/5289981.cms.

26.	Shapira S, Hammond J, Cole L. Essentials Of Terror Medicine. New York: Springer Science & Business Media; 2009.

27.	Caravalho J. Dismounted complex blast injury task force; final report. Prepared for U.S. Army Surgeon General. 18 June 2011:44-47.

28.	Eastridge BJ, Mabry R, Seguin P, et al. Prehospital death on the battlefield: implications for the future of combat casualty care. *J Trauma Acute Care Surg* 2012;73:S431-S437.

29.	Anderson R, Shawen S, Kragh J, et al: Special topics. *J Am Acad Orthop Surg* 2012;20:S94-S98.

30.	Kragh JF Jr, Walters TJ, Baer DG, et al. Practical use of emergency tourniquets to stop bleeding in major limb trauma. *J Trauma* 2008 Feb;64(2 Suppl):S38-49; discussion S49-50.

31.	Kheirabadi BS, Scherer MR, Estep JS, Dubick MA, Holcomb JB. Determination of efficacy of new hemostatic dressings in a model of extremity arterial hemorrhage in swine. *J Trauma* 2009 Sep; 67(3):450-9.

32.	Kheirabadi B. Evaluation of topical hemostatic agents for combat wound treatment. *US Army Med Dep J.* 2011;Apr-Jun:25-37.

33.	*http://c\protect\unhbox\voidb@x\penalty\@M\hskip\z@skip-\discretionary{}{}{}\penalty\ @M\hskip\z@skip{}tecc.org/images/content/TECC_Guidelines_DEC_2014_update.pdf.*

34.	*https://www.naemt.org/education/TCCC/guidelines_curriculum.*

35.   *E.M. Bulger, et al. Prehospital Guidelines for External Hemorrhage Control. Prehospital Emergency Care. 2014. 18:163-173.*

36.   National Institute of Justice. Selection and Application Guide to Personal Body Armor. Washington, DC: U.S. Department of Justice; 2001.

37.   Montanarelli N, Hawkins CE, Goldfarb MA, Ciurej TF. Protective Garments for Public Officials. Aberdeen Proving Ground, MD: U.S. Army Land Warefare Laboratory;1973.

38.   Hanlon E, Gillich P. Origin of the 44-mm Behind-Armor Blunt Trauma Standard. *Military Medicine* 2012;177 (333-339).

39.   Montanarelli N, et al. *Protective Garments for Public Officials.*

40.   Department of Justice. NILECJ Standard on the Ballistic Resistance of Police Body Armor. Washington, D.C.: U.S. Department of Justice, Law Enforcement Assitance Administration, National Criminal Justice Reference Service; 1972. — — —. Supplement I: Status Report to the Attorney General on Body Armor. U.S. Department of Justice Office of Justice Programs National Institute of Justice Safety Initiative Testing and Activities. In Special Report: NIJ; 2004. — — —. NIJ Standards: Ballistic Resistance of Body Armor, NIH Standard-0101.06; 2008.

41.   Department of Justice. NIJ Standards: Ballistic Resistance of Body Armor, NIH Standard-0101.06; 2008.

42.   U.S. Congress, Office of Technology Assessment, *Police Body Armor Standards and Testing, Volume II: Appendices*, OTA-ISC-535. Washington, DC: U.S. Government Printing Office; 1992.

43.   National Institute of Justice. Selection and Application Guide to Personal Body Armor. Washington, DC: U.S. Department of Justice; 2001.

44.   National Institute of Justice. Standard-0101.06, Ballistic Resistance of Body Armor. https://www.ncjrs.gov/pdffiles1/nij/223054.pdf.

45.   Department of Justice. Bulletproof Vest Partnership/ Body Armor Safety Initiative. 2010. http://www.ojp.usdoj.gov/bvpbasi/award_reports/2010vests.html.

46.   Salomone JP, Pons PT, McSwain NE. eds. *PHTLS Prehospital trauma life support:Military 7th ed.* St. Louis, MO: Mosby JEMS Elsevier; 2011.

47.   http://www.atec.army.mil/foia.html

48.   *http://www.usfa.fema.gov/downloads/pdf/publications/active_shooter_guide.pdf.*

49.   *http://www.iafc.org/files/1ASSOC/IAFCPosition_ActiveShooterEvents.pdf.*

50.   *http://www.iaff.org/Comm/PDFs/IAFF_Active_Shooter_Position_Statement.pdf.*

51.   *http://www.usfa.fema.gov/downloads/pdf/publications/active_shooter_guide.pdf.*

52.   *http://www.usfa.fema.gov/downloads/pdf/publications/active_shooter_guide.pdf.*

53.   *http://www.iaff.org/Comm/PDFs/IAFF_Active_Shooter_Position_Statement.pdf.*

54.   *Wound Data and Munitions Effectiveness Team. The WDMET Study, Bethesda; Uniformed Services University of the Health Sciences; 1970.*

55.   *http://www.fema.gov/national\protect\unhbox\voidb@x\penalty\@M\hskip\z@skip-\discretionary{}{}{}\penalty\@M\hskip\z@skip{}incident\protect\unhbox\voidb@x\penalty\@M\hskip\z@skip-\discretionary{}{}{}\penalty\@M\hskip\z@skip{}management\protect*

unhbox\voidb@x\penalty\@M\hskip\z@skip-\discretionary{}{}{}\penalty\@M\hskip\z@skip{}system.

56.   *http://www.fema.gov/national\protect\unhbox\voidb@x\penalty\@M\hskip\z@skip-\discretionary{}{}{}\penalty\@M\hskip\z@skip{}response\protect\unhbox\voidb@x\penalty\@M\hskip\z@skip-\discretionary{}{}{}\penalty\@M\hskip\z@skip{}framework.*

57.   *Blast injuries are the result of the rapid chemical conversion of a solid or liquid into highly pressurized gasses that expand rapidly and compress the surrounding air. This generates a pressure pulse, which spreads as a blast wave in all directions. The effects of the blast wave are more intense in a confined space like a building or bus. The shock wave is amplified as it is reflected off walls, floors, and the ceiling. If the blast occurs outside, the blast wave will dissipate rapidly. It is understood that over-pressure phenomena may enhance the lethality of blast effect for explosions that occur in confined spaces.*

58.   *Blast injuries are the result of the rapid chemical conversion of a solid or liquid into highly pressurized gasses that expand rapidly and compress the surrounding air. This generates a pressure pulse, which spreads as a blast wave in all directions. The effects of the blast wave are more intense in a confined space like a building or bus. The shock wave is amplified as it is reflected off walls, floors, and the ceiling. If the blast occurs outside, the blast wave will dissipate rapidly. It is understood that over-pressure phenomena may enhance the lethality of blast effect for explosions that occur in confined spaces.*

59.   *Blast injuries are the result of the rapid chemical conversion of a solid or liquid into highly pressurized gasses that expand rapidly and compress the surrounding air. This generates a pressure pulse, which spreads as a blast wave in all directions. The effects of the blast wave are more intense in a confined space like a building or bus. The shock wave is amplified as it is reflected off walls, floors, and the ceiling. If the blast occurs outside, the blast wave will dissipate rapidly. It is understood that over-pressure phenomena may enhance the lethality of blast effect for explosions that occur in confined spaces.*

60.   *Blast injuries are the result of the rapid chemical conversion of a solid or liquid into highly pressurized gasses that expand rapidly and compress the surrounding air. This generates a pressure pulse, which spreads as a blast wave in all directions. The effects of the blast wave are more intense in a confined space like a building or bus. The shock wave is amplified as it is reflected off walls, floors, and the ceiling. If the blast occurs outside, the blast wave will dissipate rapidly. It is understood that over-pressure phenomena may enhance the lethality of blast effect for explosions that occur in confined spaces.*

61.   *Blast injuries are the result of the rapid chemical conversion of a solid or liquid into highly pressurized gasses that expand rapidly and compress the surrounding air. This generates a pressure pulse, which spreads as a blast wave in all directions. The effects of the blast wave are more intense in a confined space like a building or bus. The shock wave is amplified as it is reflected off walls, floors, and the ceiling. If the blast occurs outside, the blast wave will dissipate rapidly. It is understood that over-pressure phenomena may enhance the lethality of blast effect for explosions that occur in confined spaces.*

62.   Department of Justice. Bulletproof Vest Partnership / Body Armor Safety Initiative. 2010. http://www.ojp.usdoj.gov/bvpbasi/award_reports/2010vests.html

63.   Salomone JP, Pons PT, McSwain NE. eds. *PHTLS Prehospital trauma life support: Military 7th ed.* St. Louis, MO: Mosby JEMS Elsevier; 2011.

64.   Department of Justice. Bulletproof Vest Partnership / Body Armor Safety Initiative. 2010. http://www.ojp.usdoj.gov/bvpbasi/award_reports/2010vests.html

65. Salomone JP, Pons PT, McSwain NE. eds. *PHTLS Prehospital trauma life support: Military 7th ed.* St. Louis, MO: Mosby JEMS Elsevier; 2011.

66. Department of Justice. Bulletproof Vest Partnership / Body Armor Safety Initiative. 2010. http://www.ojp.usdoj.gov/bvpbasi/award_reports/2010vests.html

67. Salomone JP, Pons PT, McSwain NE. eds. *PHTLS Prehospital trauma life support: Military 7th ed.* St. Louis, MO: Mosby JEMS Elsevier; 2011.

www.ingramcontent.com/pod-product-compliance
Lightning Source LLC
Chambersburg PA
CBHW051741250726
48659CB00001B/182